Best Damn Life Workbook

Risa J. Stein, PhD

BDL Publishing

Risa@GenuineU.com

Book Layout ©2017 BookDesignTemplates.com

Ordering Information:

Quantity sales. Special discounts are available on quantity purchases by corporations, associations, and others. For details, contact the "Special Sales Department" at the address above.

Best Damn Life Workbook/Risa J. Stein, PhD. —1st ed.

ISBN 978-0-9856779-3-0

Contents

Best Damn Life Workbook

For Keith, my love

And, you. You know who you are
(or at least you will by the time we're done).

*"I still don't know what I was waiting for
And my time was running wild
A million dead-end streets
And every time I thought I'd got it made
It seemed the taste was not so sweet."*

– David Bowie

PREFACE

7/23/2017

I JUST RECEIVED the first round of feedback on the first draft of the first four chapters of this book. OUCH! I'm truly thankful for my friend's honest appraisal of my work and the good that will surely come from it; but, damn... I must say it stings a bit.

So, why did I bother doing this? Because the feedback from my friend will take this book in a direction that makes it much more effective and helps me develop a clearer vision of my message. Ultimately, this will make the project more personally fulfilling and gratifying.

Accepting her forthright advice is just unsettling right now.

In a nutshell, my friend said, "...define your audience better, introduce yourself earlier, and don't be such an asshole..." That last part might be tough. Of course, the intent of this book is to promote personal growth, so I'll give it my best shot.

I struggled for decades with an aversion to risk and failure. I was filled with trepidation and doubt when faced with trying something new – like writing a book. However, part of the strategy I advocate involves overcoming aversion to vulnerability, risk-taking, and failure, so I had to take the mandatory step of sharing my rough, raw first draft with people whose opinions I respected...no matter how anxiety-ridden that action was.

What my friend said was valid. If I try to understand you better and help you appreciate where I'm coming from, my message will more likely resonate with you. And, maybe if I'm not in your face about it, it will be even easier for you to listen, learn, and benefit from my approach, making this a more rewarding journey for both of us.

So, I'll share with you my personal crisis and why it was important for me to do something I've never done before. I'll introduce you to the mind demons: Impostor Syndrome, Invulnerability, Risk and Failure Aversion. And, then, we'll explore the tools I've used successfully so that you, too, can evict the demons dwelling in your head.

Who knows? Maybe you'll discover how to make yourself vulnerable to someone. Maybe you'll figure out what brings you happiness and a sense of fulfillment. And, just maybe, you'll forge a path you can call your own and, like me, craft a masterpiece for the ages.

Risa

~~~~~~~~~~~~~~~~~~~

You want to live your best damn life.

It's natural though for a life path that provided fulfillment at one stage to require re-evaluation when priorities and desires change. Shifts in values can occur when you reach milestones such as entering the workforce, starting a family, or retiring. Or, you might simply awaken one day feeling like a stranger on a predictable and stifling journey.

The key, in any scenario, is to recognize the need for realignment of a life path to your current priorities, values, and desires and, rather than fearing the process or denying it altogether, to approach it as an exciting opportunity.

Getting started

Any beneficial form of therapy will be supported by research. This book abides by the same principle. The problem I encountered in writing *Best Damn Life Workbook* is that there is isn't a lot of research on constructing or redesigning a life path. So, I worked with what I could find on topics such as anxiety, depression, decision-making, and relationships and created one for us.

I have intentionally designed this book as a guide – a user's manual, of sorts. Many of the exercises I've developed, and the structure I employ to help you create your path, have a foundation in scientific literature. While I won't go into detail about the research behind my approach, I realize you may be interested in further exploration of certain areas. So, I've peppered the workbook with references to other books and videos that helped me clarify my perspective, and that you might enjoy, as well.

While therapy based on research is most effective, the protocol must still be tailored to the person attempting to create change. That's why you'll find so many "fill-in-the-blank" exercises in *Best Damn Life*. The method is based on scientific findings, but the approach is personalized to you.

Best Damn Life Workbook is divided into three main parts. Each part covers a different aspect of life path development.

Part 1 concentrates on understanding how and why you've dug your life hole rather than creating a scenic path.

As you grew and matured, your actions were guided by those around you. These folks were likely benevolent adults who aimed to make you a productive member of society. They praised and punished you in ways intended to help you conform and succeed. As you grew, you continued to trust in and operate under their guidelines.

Unfortunately, it's nearly impossible to know how to best tailor a complete life path to a child. Ultimately, following society's messages and guidelines can create a disconnect from your most authentic journey. Rather than moving you forward, society's one-size-fits-all messages become shovels. Each time you internalize messages about what others think is best for you, you dig yourself into a deeper hole.

Forging a fulfilling life path requires you gain an understanding of the impact these messages have on your approach to life.

In Part 2, the focus is on understanding the embodiment of these messages - the "mind demons."

Accumulated societal messages eventually take on lives of their own. They become aversions to vulnerability, risk, and failure along with impostor syndrome. These four mindsets – or mind demons - limit your ability to align yourself with a meaningful life path.

To move forward you must create a new mindset and perspective that won't control and limit you the way the mind demons have.

Part 3 introduces ways to conceptualize and begin constructing a fulfilling life path.

Once barriers are removed, the realization of a wide-open horizon can be overwhelming. You may decide to meander a while and see the many sights you previously missed out on. Or, you may wish to jump right in and determine your true north. Either way, you'll assess what you'd value most from your new path and begin construction of a route aligned with your authentic self. All the understanding and personal insights gained from Parts 1 and 2 will be put to use in Part 3 as you initiate meaningful change.

If you feel stymied or as though your life no longer fits you, or if you find yourself at a crossroad, a dead end, or stuck in a hole, you need tools to help you discern a new path. Let this book serve as your guide in deciphering the path best tailored to you.

This is where your journey begins.

Part 1

DIGGING A HOLE

CHAPTER 1

The hole

HERE YOU GO!

Maybe you have put off thinking about or creating positive change in your life or you've thought seriously about it and come up dry. A fresh perspective can clarify how you've reached this stuck point. Once you understand how the hole you've found yourself in was dug, the mindset protecting it, and how to destroy the wall surrounding it, you can begin to create a new perspective and construct your personally-tailored, fulfilling path.

For demonstration purposes, let's first consider the radical approach presented in the *Seinfeld* episode where George Costanza does the opposite of every instinct he has:

> *"It's not working, Jerry. It's just not working.*
>
> *When did it all turn out like this for me? I had so much promise. I was personable. I was bright. Oh, maybe not academically speaking. I was perceptive. I always know when someone's uncomfortable at a party.*
>
> *It all became very clear to me sitting out there today. Every decision I've ever made in my entire life is the complete opposite of everything I want it to be. Every instinct I have in every aspect of life, be it something to wear, something to eat... it's all been wrong. Every one."*[1]

---

[1] Seinfeld, May 19, 1994. Season 5, Episode 22, "The Opposite"

You probably know where this goes. Instead of ordering tuna on toast, George orders "chicken salad on rye, untoasted, with a side of potato salad and a cup of tea." And, with this lunch order and new approach, his life changes.

You can change your life, too. Not likely as a result of changing your lunch order, but certainly that's a starting point.

George may have been better served in the long-run by considering what he really wanted out of life, but he wasn't fearful of running small experiments - such as changing his lunch order - which can provide useful insights.

The experiments serve another purpose, too. Humans operate on feedback loops - change your behavior, and your frame of reference and mindset shift. Change your mindset, and your behavior follows suit. You can see this with George, as his new-found authenticity boosts his confidence and alters his perspective on life.

Although poorly contrived or executed plans are rarely devastating - thoughtful plans, considerate of, aligned with, and built upon a foundation of self-knowledge - are truly life enhancing. Across the next several chapters, you'll work through exercises designed to help you create a mindset conducive to climbing out of the hole and embarking on a satisfying life path.

Where to begin?

When you are just starting out on your own how are you to truly know what you want? After a lifetime of work and care for others, how are you to know which retirement plan will best suit you? Once you find yourself stuck in a stifling existence, how are you to know where to turn?

Whether you are contemplating your post-high school, post-college, or post-career future; or, you've hit a wall in your job or life in general, you can create a fulfilling path.

The key is to identify and remove obstacles that block your appreciation of your genuine self and what you value and enjoy. Once the obstacles are removed, you'll be observant enough to note when additional modifications are warranted and agile enough to continually modify your approach to life.

Life shovels

The first step for creating change involves gaining insight. You'll need a level of understanding that provides a foothold before you start to climb out of your hole.

When you review your past patterns of interactions, you'll likely realize that you didn't simply find yourself in a hole. Along the way, you received certain messages meant to shape your behavior to align with societal expectations. You were given shovels and you set about digging.

People typically take this action without conscious recognition of what they're doing - just following directions and performing as instructed.

Take a look at the following list of statements, which constitute shovels, and just nod if any have been directed at you:

- Sit down and shut up.
- Only the rare few ever accomplish their dreams, be realistic.
- Make a mistake and you're done for.
- Play it safe or you could lose everything.
- Be happy with what you have, others have so much less.
- Don't rock the boat.
- Quit asking so many questions, it's annoying.
- Just trust me.
- Change is scary.
- What? You think you're special?
- Just do as instructed and everything will be fine.
- Stop complaining.
- That's a dumb idea.
- Just try to fit in.
- Stay between the lines.
- Children should be seen and not heard.

- Slow and steady wins the race.
- Quit being such a bitch.
- That's been done already.
- Just sit still, for crying out loud.
- What's your plan B?
- Is this really the best you can do?
- Why can't you be more like your brother/sister?
- Who do you think you are?
- Did you really think that would work?
- Because I said so.
- But, everyone does it this way.
- It's not your turn.
- Take the blue pill.

What do those statements have in common? They're all meant to keep you down, to convince you that *other people* do interesting and fantastic things. Often, well-meaning people share such sentiments to stifle what they consider unrealistic hopes and dreams, with the intention of protecting you against harsh realities.

The lemmings say them to coerce you to play along. The malicious say them to keep you from out-doing them.

Regardless, you probably heard these messages, and others, repeatedly as you grew up. You may have heard certain ones from your parents and others from your teachers. Some shovels seem to cut through the dirt with ease while others are duller and leave you hacking at the ground in what seems like a futile effort. Regardless, all the shoveling can cause you to develop a tough, calloused exterior. Or, conversely, it may have left you raw and sensitive.

Look down this list and visualize each message you've heard as a shovel scooping the earth out from under your feet. After you internalize enough of them, you'll find yourself in a hole framed by a tall dirt wall.

I have just introduced you to the origin of your life hole.

Without insight, you'll unwittingly continue to accept shovel 'statements' throughout your life. After a while, you'll unconsciously adapt to and accept the confines you've created as a result of all your digging. Since you rarely get to glimpse over the wall, you have no awareness of life beyond the hole you've dug. Eventually, you simply live in accordance with the limitations set by your various 'shovels'.

Grit and growth

Often the hole-digging messages come packaged in unwittingly discouraging experiences that can exert a tremendous impact on your outlook on life.

Say you and a classmate each received a "D" on a fourth-grade math test. When returning the tests, your math teacher might have insinuated that math just isn't your thing while your classmate was told to just try harder.

Experiences like these promote the development of what psychologist Carol Dweck refers to as a "fixed" or a "growth" mindset. A fixed-mindset suggests that you have all the talent, skill, intelligence, and ability you'll ever have right now.

So, if your teacher tells you that math "isn't your thing," she's subtly insinuating that you'll likely never perform better than D-level work in math. Your math teacher promoted a "fixed" mindset by suggesting that math isn't for you and there's really nothing you can do about it. Why should you even bother working harder when your potential is fixed and limited?

The hole-digging fixed-mindset creeps, too. While the math test you performed poorly on may have been specific to fractions, all the sudden, in your mind, you're 100% bad at math. And, it gets worse. From now on, every math test you take will cause you anxiety. You'll go into the test primed to fail "knowing" math isn't your thing. Thereafter, every test becomes a self-fulfilling prophecy confirming your inability to do math.

That's the power these messages have on limiting your perspective on life. What are you to do now if you are fascinated by the stars and really want to become an astronomer? Given the level of math and physics involved in that field, you'll probably view yourself as incapable and give up on the dream.

On the other hand, your teacher promoted a "growth" mindset in your classmate through encouraging her to expect better results if she put forth greater effort. There's still hope for her. The ball is in her court and she can grow and progress if she only works at. Sure, she might still perform poorly now and then on difficult math tests, but she knows her grades are not reflective of who she is and what she's capable of achieving. So, she soldiers on!

Dr. Dweck suggests, and I really love this, that a fixed-mindset says, "I'm not good at math" while a growth-mindset says, "I'm not good at math, yet."

It's amazing the difference one little three-letter word makes in your outlook on life: YET – there's magic in "yet." *Yet* offers hope. *Yet* provides a reason to keep going when you doubt yourself. *Yet* promotes resilience.

And, *yet* creates what Dr. Angela Duckworth identifies as "grit." Grit is necessary for you to forge ahead in the face of adversity and to ultimately reach your goals.

To hear more about the "fixed" versus "growth" mindset and the value of "grit" listen to Dr. Dweck's TED talk, "The power of believing you can improve" and Dr. Duckworth's TED talk, "Grit: The power of passion and perseverance." Both have also written outstanding books.

If you are working through one of life's stuck points, consider the source of your emotional angst. For most of us, this comes from the feeling that we have played a role that no longer suits us. You too, may yearn to break free and redefine yourself in a new role, but contemplating this change may make you fearful and anxious, and you might question whether you have what it takes to climb from your hole and walk that new path. Your anxiety, at least in part, is the result of adopting a fixed-mindset which leaves you feeling stymied.

Not knowing the best way to free/recreate/redefine yourself and your future, of feeling antsy — as though something greater is under your skin trying to escape — is frustrating. You've obviously been down in that hole for far too long.

Most people, when stuck in a hole, scratch at the sides in attempt to escape. You probably haven't sat idly by your whole life, only to awaken one day feeling uncomfortable. Instead, you likely fought and fought — sometimes small battles, sometimes large, valiant ones. After a time, though, you've developed a sense of hopelessness and slipped back into a fixed-mindset. Then the struggle began to feel futile and the wall insurmountable.

You've probably heard that the first law of being in a hole is to stop digging.

That's great. But what are you supposed to do if you're not digging? No one ever follows up on that cliché. Surely there is some alternative to digging that doesn't involve simply rolling over and dying? But, what?

The First Law of Holes: If you find yourself in a hole, stop digging.

Great. But, then what?

Rarely is someone else able to effectively pull you out of the hole. However, if you analyze the situation by asking targeted questions and gaining relevant insights, I believe you can figure something out on your own.

Ask-kicking

This is a good point to break and consider the ass-kicking power of asking questions. (Did you see how "asking" is just an abbreviated form of "ass-kicking"? Cool, eh?)

First, grab a pencil and let's start working on alternatives to digging deeper or rolling over and dying.

Imagine yourself in a literal hole in the ground. It's 8-feet deep. You're stuck at the bottom. There's nothing down there with you except a shovel.

Now, write out five different questions you could ask about the hole you're stuck in, the shovel in your hand, or your digging strategy that might help you change this predicament. I'm being quite literal here. You're in a hole. Eight feet down. With a shovel. Ask five questions.[2]

1.

_____

_____

2.

_____

_____

3.

_____

_____

4.

_____

_____

5.

_____

_____

---

[2] A pdf version of the exercises included in the *Best Damn Life Workbook* can be found at http://www.GenuineU.org/bdlw

Here are the questions I came up with:

1. Can I keep shoveling and find someone who wants to buy the dirt?
2. If someone buys the dirt, how much beer can I buy with that money?
3. If I can buy a whole keg, can I throw a party and convince others to start shoveling dirt, too?
4. If I get ten other people to shovel dirt for two hours and three more places to buy it, that would be... 10x2x3xX$ = ... Never mind, it's beer money. How much do shovels cost?
5. Could I make the holes into pools and have an even better party?

How did your list compare with mine? Did you focus solely on ways out of the hole? Did you contemplate what you learned from being stuck in the hole? Did you find ways of making your experience in the hole pay off for you? Maybe you didn't. That's okay, for now. But maybe you'd like to come party at my place and do some digging?

Ask effective questions

Consider the differences between your questions and mine.

If you responded to the exercise by asking questions about how to get someone to help you, you've likely assumed a helpless fixed-mindset stance. You're not going anywhere until a good Samaritan walks by.

If you took a less limited approach like mine, you've demonstrated your ability to employ a growth-mindset. Now you're in control, anything is possible, and you can turn your experience into a fun, lucrative party.

See how powerful the knowledge you glean from asking effective questions from a growth-mindset can be?

It's only through asking questions that you enable yourself to understand how your hole was created, how your perspective limits you, and how you can effectively overcome these challenges to construct a new, meaningful life path.

So, what I'm saying is, get used to asking questions.

Develop a growth perspective

Asking effective questions is key to learning about yourself and forging a personally-tailored path. Without a growth perspective, you'll continue to carve away at the sides of the hole, increasing the likelihood the walls will collapse in on you.

With a perspective change, you will become increasingly comfortable with vulnerability, risk, and failure. You'll come to view setbacks as learning experiences. Rather than admitting defeat, you'll seek information about how to overcome obstacles and move forward on your life path.

You'll work on nurturing your growth perspective in the following chapters.

 From here...

As you read through each chapter, I'll continue to offer sidebars directing you to additional resources or making brief diversions from the course. Each chapter is also summarized at the end so that you can reacquaint yourself with the points you've covered. If you are holding a physical book, I strongly encourage you to mark it up and make it yours. When you read something that triggers a thought, jot it down in the margins, or in the Notes section in the back. There's a good chance you'll revisit that note later and have an epiphany. I also suggest a highlighter and colorful sticky tabs. My hope is that by the last page, this book is marked up, creased, and dog-eared. You get extra credit for coffee or tea cup rings on the pages.

If you have an electronic copy of *Best Damn Life*, I suggest you create electronic bookmarks and purchase a journal to jot your responses and thoughts down in. You will also find a pdf version of the exercises at http://www.GenuineU.com/bdlw.

For now though — grab a pillow and get comfortable.

CHAPTER 1 TRAIL MARKERS

Your limiting life perspective is formed early and creates a fixed-mindset.

The way you see the world and the possibilities it holds determines your potential.

Adopt an exploratory perspective that leads to asking insight-generating questions.

Many worlds of thought, expertise, and personal experience have formed the basis of what you'll read in the *Best Damn Life Workbook.*

CHAPTER 2

You don't know Jack

JACK IS A GREAT GUY. He's personable, athletic, and intelligent. Jack has a lovely wife he met in college and two adorable kids. After high school, Jack moved from the Midwest to a large Southern city to attend a prestigious university. He did well in school, and after graduation, went to work for a private school in an affluent nearby area.

One day, Jack turned forty and took stock of his life. Despite his intellect, good-natured personality, and boyish good looks, Jack felt unfulfilled. He was a middle administrator at the same school he began working at after college. It was great twenty years ago, but it hasn't been a good fit for quite some time.

Lately, Jack has been thinking to himself, "How did this happen? I could have – should have – amounted to so much more."

Sometimes, turning thirty (or fifty or seventy, or having a heart attack) is your wake-up call. Other times, it's graduation, the birth of a baby, or the death of a parent. It could be a depressing twenty-year class reunion or a black-tie cocktail party with snobs.

But, don't blame it on the elitists. You've finally (!) reached the point of asking, "Seriously? Is this it?"

I know, you want to cry, you want to punch something, you want to run off to Bangkok and forget it all. The realization that your life has derailed scares the bejeezus out of you. So, what are you going to do about it? Do you dare consider going for something different and completely awesome? I mean, there are no guarantees. What if you try – and then totally, completely, unequivocally, by anyone's standards fail miserably?

What if your coach/teacher/minister/ex-spouse is right about you?

Nah, they're not right. Why did you even think that? Where's your confidence?

Let me provide you a clue. If you go back in time, you can usually figure out how you lost your mojo and accepted such a confining life. If you're just embarking on a path of self-discovery and hoping to avoid the mid-life wake-up call, and the accompanying angst Jack and I experienced, consider how your life up to this point may have contributed to your consternation over future plans.

To get a better handle on this predicament, let's return to the hole-digging, wall-forming messages you received while growing up. This will constitute your first step in understanding how you ended up in a hole.

Early indoctrination

Jack's parents loved him and his siblings. They provided copious support and encouragement throughout his childhood. He progressed through school earning high marks and rewards. Jack received praise from his teachers and parents and the admiration of his peers.

He often heard how smart he was. He internalized this and understood that if he continued to do what it took to please others, and make the grades, he'd have a rosy future with a pretty wife and a white picket fence. And maybe, just maybe, if he did *really* well, a Porsche.

Then, he'd have made it and, by default, be super happy for ever after.

Jack bought into the myth and kept his head down, his nose to the grindstone, and did what was necessary to check the requisite boxes to land a coveted spot with a highly reputable university.

> *Consider the messages you received from the adults in your life while you were growing up. What expectations were placed upon you? Were you compared to your older sibling? Were you expected to follow in your father's footsteps? Were you the class clown? The student body president? The jock?*

Ta-da! Way to go, Jack! You have a bright future ahead of you, young man. But — wait! Could it be that where Jack went to college, and even whether he went to college, was predicated on something other than Jack's sincere reflection on what best suited him? Could it be that Jack simply internalized the assumption that the "best" route for smart guys like him always involved attending the best college? Could this be evidence of Jack's hole-digging behavior?

Jack clearly developed a growth-mindset around academics and realized he was a high achiever in this domain. But, what do you suppose Jack saw as the alternative to busting his butt to make the grades while following the golden path to success? Was his self-confidence as high in non-academic domains? Unlikely. Jack internalized the message that he must continue to prove his value and worth through academics. So, his life path was paved along this trajectory.

After a while, Jack came to believe that one poor grade could undermine his worth and cause his perfect house of cards to crumble. This put tremendous pressure on him to stay the course.

When Jack started college, his status as the high-achiever among his peers changed. He was surrounded by highly capable people. This scared the heck out of him, since his identity had been woven around being an academic leader and the respect he'd experienced among his peers and teachers back home.

So, Jack did what Jack had been trained to do: he dug in (and dug his hole deeper) and exceeded expectations in the classroom. It nearly became a life and death endeavor. Often, taking an exam felt like a life or death endeavor! He rarely spoke up in class for fear saying something stupid and losing the esteem of his peers and teachers.

After years spent living life perched on a precarious wire, Jack felt like he was always one false move away from disaster. But he reasoned it was only for four years. Then, he'd have cleared the first major hurdle and he'd move on to graduate school.

After that, Jack would amass the credentials to live the dream on his own terms. He assumed he'd magically be lifted out of his hole and over the wall, once he received the right diploma. After all, this was the implied message Jack had repeatedly received: "Just stick with the plan and the world will be your oyster."

So, Jack trudged along, paying his dues.

But, after college, Jack was exhausted. His nerves were frayed and he was tired of performing. He was offered an excellent job and decided to take a year off and work. He married his girlfriend; and, to their delight and surprise, they welcomed their first child a year later. Jack manned-up, put his grad school dreams on hold and worked hard to build a stable home.

The walls around his hole didn't crumble, though, when he decided to forego the continued pressure of graduate school. In fact, Jack retained the earlier admonishments and internalized additional messages about how husbands, fathers, and employees are expected to behave. And so, the hole grew deeper and the walls grew taller.

It seems clear at this point, that some, if not all, of Jack's decisions were made based on social pull. You can refer back to the list of statements at the start of the last chapter and guess which ones Jack repeatedly heard.

Fast-forward twenty years...

Jack's home is comfortable and filled with love. He has great friends, too. But he's having a hard time with what he considers his personal worth. Much of this stems from his feelings of underachievement in the workplace. He recognizes he's been fortunate in many ways and feels he has no right complain, but he can't shake the feeling that he's playing the leading role in a crappy B-movie about someone else's stifling life.

Let's look at how Jack's early path, built around meeting others' expectations, landed him in this rut.

The impact of education indoctrination

A deeper investigation of the common phenomenon Jack fell prey to reveals the subtle forces that conspired to make him a second-string player in his own life.

First and foremost, he was sucked into the education game. We spend a substantial portion of our early formative years entrenched in education. Likewise, most advanced countries set an education track for students and reward conformity. Jack was repeatedly praised for playing the game well, which meant making the grades. With this re-inforcement, he naturally became very invested in the game.

This path left little room for any sort of thoughtful deviation on Jack's part. After all, what takes place in school is often not character-ized so much as true learning, but as conditioning. Information is im-planted, typically without connection and reason. So, while Jack underwent a successful knowledge implant, he never truly learned how to learn, much less how to ask meaningful questions, or discern what truly captivated his interest. Like most of us, Jack never learned to think critically about his life path. And so, blindly, Jack commenced to digging.

"But, what the hell?" you might be saying. "I didn't make straight A's like Jack. Why are we stuck in the same hole?" Great question and kudos to you for asking!

So, maybe you were the straight "C" student. How did that feel? Demoralizing, at times? Gee, I wonder why. Could it be that your par-ents pressured you to "try harder" to "live up to your potential?" Did your teachers favor "A" students, like Jack, over you? Or, maybe you just adopted a fixed-mindset and assumed school, in general, wasn't your thing.

At what point in your education did you realize you were not a top student, and therefore, certain aspirations were supposedly off-limits for you? My guess is by around 3rd grade, you, your peers, and your teachers had a fair read of who the "smart" kids were. Teachers are generally able to discern educational talent around that point and engage in subtle (and sometimes not so subtle) interactions with students, based on these perceptions.

Did you catch my use of the term "educational talent" over intelligence or success potential? That was a deliberate choice, because successfully navigating your way through the education system does not necessarily equate to successfully navigating your way through life. Jack made straight A's and wound up with a mid-life crisis. Not everyone who makes good grades is condemned to such a future, but the rates are higher than you might think.

What Jack learned, as William Deresiewicz puts it in his book *Excellent Sheep: The miseducation of the American elite and the way to a meaningful life,* was how to jump through hoops and become one of the most "excellent sheep."

Jack was reassured that all would be well for him in life, since he exceeded the education systems standards. There's a strong lure, to be sure, for giving society what it wants.

~~~~~~~~~~~~~~~~~~~~

Rant alert: *I feel we get a significant start on digging our holes in school. It's the rare student who arrives in my psychology class day one of their freshman year of college, who is not already mired in self-doubt and mentally fatigued from digging their hole.*

One of my gripes with education is its one-size-fits-all, conveyer belt approach. After you've experienced the standardized curriculum of elementary school, it's on to middle school. After middle school, on to high school. And so on, until you've reached your ceiling, exhausted yourself, or achieved an advanced degree.

But then, what do you do with that momentum? An office on a higher floor? All for what? And, why? Who says this is the best route? All of society's drones? The peddlers of antidepressants and anxiolytics?

> *Pause here and take a moment to watch a short but highly impactful video I'll reference again later. You can find it on the internet by searching Alan Watts, "Music and life."*

What would have happened if you stopped the conveyer belt to ask what good it was going to do you to learn geometry? Maybe you did. Maybe you were that one kid in geometry class who asked why you needed to learn that stuff. If so, good for you, knock a chunk of dirt off the wall.

But, did you receive an acceptable response? Did anyone provide you an answer that put geometry into a meaningful context for you? Did you insist they teach you geometry in a way that made sense and helped you appreciate its problem-solving potential?

Or, were you just told that maybe, one day, you'd be an architect, so you should sit back down now and memorize the formula for the area of a rectangle before the school gets dinged on the standardized statewide test?

My point is, we are conditioned from an early age (refer to the list of statements at the opening of Chapter 1) to fit-in and conform, to travel down a narrowly prescribed path. If we deviate from the path due to learning disabilities, creativity, willful resistance – we are labeled outcasts and troublemakers. And, so, we are not subject to the same rewards bestowed upon those who stay the course and please the powers that be. It's a Catch-22, really. Buck the system, question the establishment, live life on your own terms and risk societal scorn or play by society's rules and risk watching the wall grow taller around your hole.

Regardless of your travels thus far, there's a good chance society has handed you a shovel and prompted you to dig a hole that ultimately restrict your view of potential life paths.

I'll step off the soap box now. Whew.

~~~~~~~~~~~~~~~~~~~~

When Jack got married, and after his first kid came along, he again accepted expectations without question. He assumed the role of primary breadwinner because that's what he was "supposed" to do. He found a good job and stuck with it for years, because that's what was best for the family. Jack decided to forgo his graduate school goals because that's what someone like Jack *should* do.

Could Jack have provided for his family *and* learned how to fulfill his dreams? Probably. Did Jack ask the questions that would have revealed various alternate paths? No, he had long ago been conditioned not to question the status quo.

And after a while, unfortunately, his hole was so deep that it negated his ability to conceive of anything different.

Another of my favorite videos, also referenced later, is one of the most popular TED talks of all time. If you'd like to hear more about the impact of the Industrial era model of education on the human capacity, watch Sir Ken Robinson's, "Do schools kill creativity?"

Assessing the damage

What did you notice about Jack's trajectory from day one?

Yup, he stayed the course. He was right on track. He performed like a rat in a maze and was periodically rewarded for doing exactly what was expected of him. He stayed in lockstep with societal expectations without ever questioning or rebelling against them. He allowed the system to define and create a future for him filled with promises of success. He assumed that success would bring him happiness and self-fulfillment. He trusted the system would come through for him. And, depending on your definition of success, many people would say that it did. After all, Jack has a nice house, a good job, a loving wife, and cute kids. Many folks would probably look enviously upon Jack and think he's got it all.

But the fact is, it's precisely because Jack so clearly met societal standards of success that he is now frustrated and confused. He asked himself why he felt like he was suffocating. He wondered what was wrong with him and why he couldn't be happy with all he had. But Jack never learned how to identify or do what would make him feel fulfilled. And now, he's lost touch with what that is. Poor sot. Jack doesn't even know Jack. Of course, he's frustrated.

He must now acquaint himself with the authentic and genuine Jack. He must remove the dirt wall from around his hole, climb out, and chart his own path if he hopes to achieve true fulfillment.

So, where's a good place for him to start?

How about at the very beginning? Redo that early programming and learn to develop a different approach to achieving success and personal fulfillment. Does Amazon sell time machines? No? Well, hell, he'll have to take a different tact.

Early on, Jack learned to follow plans others valued and dictated. He was indoctrinated and holed-in from an early age by those around him who supposedly knew what was best for him. Told that he was one of the fortunate ones, he was prodded toward a plan designed to ensure his success. However, he never asked how success would be defined or questioned the foundation of the plan.

Jack needed to begin by undoing that indoctrination - and so will you.

Not sure how this can happen? Well, here's a hint, it involves re-discovering yourself.

Before you can develop an honest, personalized, and fulfilling definition of success, you must climb out of your hole and re-learn what truly brings you satisfaction. You'll build a new perspective, ask new questions, and develop new behaviors.

So, find a relaxing spot, grab a cup of tea or coffee, and read on.

Determining your True North

To ensure your path goes where you truly want it to go, you need to continually learn about yourself and the possibilities the world holds for you. The world doesn't remain static; so, neither can you. It's really awe inspiring to know that an ever-changing world provides an endless supply of new possibilities every day.

To take advantage of all the world has to offer, it is first crucial that you understand and thoroughly appreciate that learning is an on-going process, not a destination. If you stay in place and dig, you just create a deeper hole. If you remain agile, you'll forge a path.

Say it with me now: "Forward momentum requires constant learning. Learning is a process, not a destination."

You know what? Write it on the back of your hand, so you see it every day.

Learning is a process, not a destination.

Better yet, get a tattoo. No, never mind. Don't get a tattoo. Well, unless you really want a tattoo, in which case – go for it!

You're not in seventh grade anymore. Learning isn't perfunctory. It should have meaning. It should add quality to your life. But let's be clear, without engagement in the process of learning, you will never... say that out loud... NEVER climb out of that hole.

In fact, let's up the ante a bit. You must engage in learning, for learning's sake. You are not going to learn on a prn (only as needed) basis. You are going to learn because it destroys the helpless, confined animal mindset. It opens doors.

You might not know where any specific learning will lead you, but each new fact learned, experience encountered, experiment conducted, and person met, moves you a step closer to the hallowed ground that is nowhere near that spot you're stuck in.

To remain agile like a ninja or Navy SEAL, you can't kick back in your Lay-Z-Boy chair and read books or watch other ninjas on YouTube. You need to become a part of the action. You need to have skin in the game. If you're passively allowing yourself to be taught, then you're not really committed. You're just following the original script that resulted in your feeling stuck. That's why this is a workbook, not a regular read-through-and-set-aside book. Hooyah? Hooyah!!

 From here...

I've presented several steps for moving past your stuck point and creating a new path for yourself. Before you jump out and start barreling through walls though, let's take inventory of your current armament. Could it be you're better prepared than you realized? Could it be you have big guns, but no ammo? Or, could it be that you're essentially standing naked in front of the firing line? Wherever you are, you'll move forward from YOUR starting point.

Need another cup of coffee? Take a break and grab a pen.

CHAPTER 2 TRAIL MARKERS

Society has likely influenced the way you view your potential life path.

Consider your definition of success and your assumptions on how to achieve it.

Learning is a process, not a destination.

Thoughtful questioning will guide you out of your hole.

CHAPTER 3

Make a PACT

BEFORE YOU MOVE forward, I want to offer you an opportunity to formally commit to creating your fulfilling life path. Your motivation may waver when the process becomes challenging. For many folks, committing in writing to an undertaking bolsters their resolve. You don't have to sign it to undergo personal growth, but if you're like me, signing your name to something provides traction for moving forward.

I, (print your name) _____, make a pact with myself to engage in a process of self-discovery. I will ask questions and remain open to learning more about myself through experimentation and exploration. I will engage in thoughtful reflection on my experiences and I will apply my curiosity to create new ones. I will use the exercises in this book to help me create an authentic, meaningful, and fulfilling life path.

_____

Signature

You can sign it in pen or blood. Your choice.

Stein

This is a commitment you are making with yourself. Before moving ahead, take a quick assessment. It will help you evaluate your strengths and weaknesses. Last thing you want to do is fall prey to the manipulative voices telling you to skate by and slack off on some of the finer points. Creating a well-suited path for yourself requires covering all your bases.

Oh, and here's a little more about that pact you just signed...

It represents the steps required to climb out of the hole and forge a new path. After you complete the assessment, I'll get more specific on how to focus on the Process of learning and exploration by becoming an Active participant driven by Curiosity in a Thoughtful manner. Yup, that's the PACT you signed.

First things first, though. Take the following assessment, and then I'll introduce you to the obstacles that limit your vision as you attempt to create a more meaningful life. Your strengths are irrelevant, if you run head-first into an obstacle that causes you to fall back into your hole every time you attempt to proceed.

PACT Assessment

Take a few minutes and honestly (!) rate yourself from 1 to 3 on the following items.

1 = NOT REALLY TRUE FOR ME
2 = SOMEWHAT TRUE FOR ME
3 = VERY TRUE FOR ME

<u>Score</u>

1. I enjoy the journey of learning even more than the destination _____

2. I often apply what I know in one area to other areas _____

3. I notice things going on around me that others don't _____

4. I build upon what I already know to deepen my knowledge _____

5. I listen to understand rather than to respond _____

6. I find ways to put new information into action _____

7. I ask follow-up questions when I'm presented with new information _____

8. I don't beat myself up when I don't understand something _____

9. I value creating positive change over attaining a specific goal or endpoint _____

<u>Score</u>

10. I actively seek out new challenges   _____

11. I enjoy exploring and learning in a physical,
    hands-on way   _____

12. I can critically evaluate the content of new
    information I receive   _____

13. I remain flexible in my purpose for learning   _____

14. I seek answers through various channels
    and resources   _____

15. I enjoy doing things I've never done before   _____

16. I can critically evaluate the source of new
    information I receive   _____

17. I do not believe my IQ dictates my ability
    to learn   _____

18. I am comfortable asking for help when I
    don't know how to do something   _____

19. I seek out various perspectives when I
    have a decision to make   _____

20. I recognize the balance between challenge and
    comfort that constitutes my learning zone   _____

To determine your strengths and weaknesses, total your responses as follows:

Process-orientation: Add together your responses to questions 1, 5, 9, 13, 17

      Total P score: _____

Action-orientation: Add together your responses to questions 2, 6, 10, 14, 18

      Total A score: _____

Curiosity: Add together your responses to questions 3, 7, 11, 15, 19

      Total C score: _____

Thoughtfulness: Add together your responses to questions 4, 8, 12, 16, 20

      Total T score: _____

How did you fare? Higher on one domain than others? About equal on all four?

You'll use this as a frame of reference and a guide as you progress.

If your score in any one area falls between 5 and 8, consider that an underdeveloped area. If your score is between 9 and 12, consider yourself about average in that area. If your score falls between 13 and 15, then congrats, you excel in this area! Even with this score, I still suggest you read through the material and then focus greater attention on the areas where your blades are not quite as sharp.

Put your shovel down

Regardless of your score, this next step will constitute your starting point. You'll work to develop your ability to Actively participate in the Process of learning. Doing so aids in the connection of new information (which you glean by asking questions) to pre-existing information. By now, you know how important asking questions is to create and sustain momentum toward developing a fulfilling life path.

You know how the world is wonderous and exciting when you're three-years-old? It can be difficult to recapture that outlook when you're twenty-three or forty-three or sixty-three. By then, the years have taken their toll. So, your first goal is to revive that three-year-old you – by reinitiating the process of asking 'why?'. And why are you going to do that? Let me tell you why...

Reason #1: Asking questions makes you an active learner

What's the real ass-kicking utility of asking questions? Asking questions serves multiple purposes - although you may have lost sight of this, as many people do.

First, it makes you an Active participant in learning. To ask good questions, you must pay attention. You must search for something that makes the information valuable, and then figure out how it fits with your pre-existing information.

Don't be lazy! If you're lazy, you're complacent. And, complacency equates to remaining frozen at the dead end or crossroad, trapped in the confines of your hole.

Reason #2: Asking questions helps you identify others willing to help

Second, asking questions signals to others that you are willing to learn. As a bonus, it helps you weed out those who don't want to see you improve yourself from those willing to help you get out of your hole.

Have you ever been in a training seminar where one person keeps asking questions, while everyone else seethes, because they just want to get out of there and go home? Maybe you were that seething person. If so, ask yourself why.

I'll venture a guess why. You were aggravated because you weren't invested in learning. You were satisfied with just putting in your time, and then going home to sit on your couch and watch TV.

In the meantime, Judy from Accounting was gaining a deeper appreciation of the material being taught. The bosses took note of her involvement and desire to grasp the information. When time came for a promotion requiring the acquisition of new material, the executive board naturally thought of Judy – even though you have greater time served in the organization. Did you ask why they chose Judy over you? Nope. Due to your mindset, you just stewed over the seeming unfairness of it all.

Reason #3: Asking questions strengthens and deepens your level of understanding

Asking questions provides a third benefit. Your questions will address gaps in your understanding. By filling in those gaps, you strengthen and deepen your understanding of a phenomenon. By connecting new information with pre-existing information, you create a cross-reference. Essentially, you have now Velcro-ed the new information into your brain by creating multiple loops and hooks from it to other established facts and experiences. Now, you can reference that information easily in a multitude of different situations. Not only will that impress your colleagues, but it makes you more creative. And you need to think creatively to escape from your rut.

If you ask questions and find ways to make learning in one domain relevant to other domains, that information becomes multi-dimensional, stronger, and more useful.

Asking questions → Learning in hyperdrive

Consider the building of a gingerbread house. Who would likely have the sturdiest and most beautiful house: Jane, a baker, John, an architect, or James, an artist?

That's a trick question. Relying solely on their unidimensional knowledge and skill set, each individual's gingerbread house would likely fall short. But, how do you suppose a house created by Jennifer, a nurse, would turn out if she possessed curiosity and a modicum of knowledge in each of the three domains?

While you've undoubtedly heard that "a little knowledge is a dangerous thing," I humbly request you challenge that axiom and change it to read: "knowledge in only one area is a dangerous thing." When coupled with a desire to learn, a little knowledge is far from dangerous!

This is a circular conundrum, though. You see, if you don't know or don't acknowledge what you don't know, then you can't ask effective problem-solving and life-enhancing questions. To maximize your impact, you need to honestly take stock of what you know along with your limitations.

Fortunately for Jennifer, she knows a little about all three gingerbread-house-building-related areas. She also knows enough to realize there are unaddressed gaps in her knowledge base. Through her limited appreciation of all three areas, Jennifer recognizes that the intersections of baking, architecture, and design are where the really great gingerbread-house-making info lies. She realizes that combined knowledge is more useful than siloed knowledge.

Creatively combining knowledge provides intellectual synergistic goodness like the deliciousness Reece's cups provide that neither chocolate or peanut butter in isolation could ever yield.

Only by considering the intersection of baking and architecture will Jennifer account for the pre- vs. post-baking shape and fit of the pieces. Wouldn't the intersection of design, baking, and architecture also lead her to question and experiment with the thickness of her icing and how it would look as cement for the walls and decorative candies? Clearly, Jennifer would ask herself intersection questions before baking, constructing, and decorating her house that Jane, John, and James might never have conceived of, given their reliance on unidimensional thinking.

Considering gingerbread house creating from multiple perspectives ultimately results in fortification of cookie walls, as well as personal skills, not to mention a more beautiful and creative finished product.

Even though Jennifer's gingerbread house construction benefitted from her previous curiosity about the three relevant areas, she didn't likely begin her exploration of any of those domains with the intention of one day creating an astounding gingerbread house. Nevertheless, her limited experience in each area provided insights and served as a compass, pointing her to sources of additional information that she could then incorporate and apply to fortify her understanding, and produce a positive outcome.

You just never know what interesting doors your knowledge can unlock!

Consider a skill you possess. What sorts of questions did you have to ask as you developed that skill? What questions could you ask to gain additional perspectives that would fortify your learning and make your skill even more impressive and valuable?

As an aside, think back to the first exercise I had you complete where you asked five questions about getting out of your hole. Remember how your questions were focused on the hole and mine involved selling dirt, buying beer, and creating pools?

It's the broader and integrated view of a problem that promotes forward movement down a path with entertaining pit stops along the way. I'm going to continue this theme in later chapters because disjointed knowledge, especially about yourself, is never as satisfying as combined and integrated knowledge.

Let's take this line of reasoning one step farther...

Suppose Jennifer decided to construct a gingerbread house in the image of St. Patrick's Cathedral in New York City. Although her previous architectural knowledge may have been restricted to post-modern works, she can now assess the neo-Gothic style from an architectural and decorative sense.

In order to bake a rendition of the famous Roman Catholic church, Jennifer recognizes the gaps in her knowledge and asks informed questions that will ultimately enhance her appreciation of this style. The new information she gleans is easily incorporated, because she has previous rudimentary architectural and design Velcro-loops to which the new architectural and design learning hooks can be linked.

In the field of computer science, this potential for exponential growth in connections is referred to as neural network creation. The more you learn and connect new learning to previous learning, the stronger and more complex your network of neural connections becomes. This pertains not only to impersonal content, but to self-knowledge, as well. In fact, the computer science folks relate the creation of complex neural networks to "deep learning."

Before you embark on creating your fulfilling life path, you're going to focus on deep learning about YOU!

The essential role of curiosity

Remember when I mentioned that you were going to start asking questions like a three-year-old?

Why is it that little kids ask so many questions, and adults not so much? Sure, they have more to learn, but do we know everything once we complete our formal education or hit fifty? Of course, we don't. So, why aren't we as persistent with our inquiries now as we were at age three?

I think the answer is two-fold.

First, as an artifact of our experiences in the education system, we just aren't as curious. And even if we do retain our sense of curiosity, we sure as heck don't want anyone to know we don't know something!

I see this in my students at the start of every semester. I tell them, "You are here to learn. Learning involves – no – requires, that you ask questions." Yet even with this guidance, it's always some time before they feel comfortable doing so. They worry about being wrong and judged by their peers. They are terribly concerned that everyone in the room is more intelligent than they and speaking up will demonstrate their cognitive inferiority.

Rest assured, you're going to kill this tendency before you're done.

To create a beautiful and life-affirming path, you must become proficient at learning and applying what you learn. I think you probably know by now how you're going to accomplish this. Yup, by asking questions. And, how do you start asking more questions? By stoking curiosity. *Curiosity* is key. Curiosity kills the status quo.

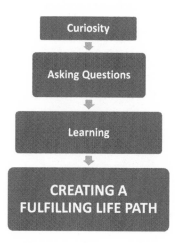

Once you've asked pertinent questions and combined disparate bits of information in your brain, you can begin conducting small experiments to advance your learning.

For instance, what would happen if I ask the girl across the hall out on a date, like the dude did in the movie I just watched? What would it be like to spend an entire Saturday with no electronic technology like they did in the olden days? What happens if I play MasterChef and mix quinoa with couscous?

Put the pedal to the metal

Now, it's your turn. Finish the simple question below:

What would happen if I... _____

_____

_____

_____.

You don't have to answer it right now, I just want to get your mind in questioning mode. But, if you'd like to investigate, by all means, do so! Maybe you'll cure cancer. Maybe you'll blow up the garage. Either way, you've become more involved in the *Process* of learning by *Actively* asking questions that exercise your *Curiosity*. Good for you!!! You are well on your way to climbing out of the hole.

Don't drive in circles

Finally, aside from valuing the Process of learning over the destination, increasing Active engagement through asking questions, and allowing your learning process to be governed by Curiosity, you need to assure you are a *Thoughtful* learner.

If Judy from Accounting is truly asking inane questions, she's not going to get ahead at work. Instead, she's going to irritate her bosses and get herself fired. The key is to ask thoughtful questions.

Mrs. Jones, your delightful second-grade teacher, who made personalized Valentines for every student, may have taught you that there are no stupid questions. Well, there may not be "stupid" questions, but there certainly are more and less productive and effective questions. If you repeatedly ask nonproductive questions, you're not engaging in learning and exploration. You're also not allowing others to engage their curiosity. What's worse, if you're incorporating dribble into your brain at face value, you're inviting misinformation and clutter to rent valuable real estate.

Let curiosity guide your learning, but let it also promote critical thinking.

From here...

I'm going to ask you to start doing some soul-searching from this point on through various exercises and experiments. There is space in this book to write your responses after every exercise. However, I would strongly encourage you to invest in a notebook or journal. Writing your thoughts in a dedicated journal will give your mind more room to wander and expound upon your curiosity. It is my expectation that your thoughts will begin to flow more freely now; so, it will be in your best interest to take note of and value them.

CHAPTER 3 TRAIL MARKERS

Asking questions allows you to build upon previous learning and effectively incorporate new information.

Commit to focusing on the Process of learning and exploration by becoming an Active participant, driven by Curiosity in a Thoughtful manner.

Regardless of your starting point, you can pave a scenic and fulfilling path.

PART 2

SLAYING THE MIND DEMONS

Meet the mind demons

MARIN, TWENTY-FIVE YEARS OLD, completed high school despite getting pregnant her junior year. Since then, she's lived with her child at her parents' house. They helped watch baby Christine while Marin went through a vocational training program after high school, and until the little girl began school. Once Marin completed her vocational training, she began working as an office assistant at a large firm. She's diligent, competent, responsible, and conscientious. Her bosses love her and she enjoys her job.

Recently, Marin was promoted to a higher-level administrative assistant position. She now supervises others and reports to a division VP in her firm. Everything has been going great for Marin, and she's finally able to consider moving out of her parents' home.

Although she thinks she could streamline several office procedures and probably save her firm some big bucks, she can't bring herself to speak up. Much of the time, rather than ask those she supervises to complete their work, Marin does it herself.

She worries about taking care of her child and not being a good enough parent; she worries about keeping her bosses satisfied with her work; and she worries about her subordinates liking her. In fact, Marin worries so much, she wakes up in a pool of sweat at least three nights a week.

Marin tries to tell herself this thought process is ridiculous. She knows her bosses value her services. And yet, there is a voice in the back of her mind that tells her she's not as good as the other employees and doesn't deserve her status or position. She hears it mock her when she considers suggesting a procedural change. It tells her to stop being "uppity" and to *remember she barely graduated high school. It tells her that if she speaks up, the others will find out she really isn't very smart, and they'll laugh at her.*

This inner voice warns her that with one misstep, she'll probably be fired. It constantly reminds her that she's a high school grad, and nothing more. A single mother, still living in her parents' home, who should recognize her place in the food chain.

Recently, Marin has wondered if she'll ever amount to anything her daughter can be proud of.

Before you get rolling on the PACT, you need to be forewarned about the mind demons keeping you paralyzed. They're the ones who block the light and prevent you from finding your way out of the hole. They represent echoes of the voices heard during your formative years. They've set up shop in your mind and act like snipers, stealthy and lethal.

Through the course of your maturation and indoctrination, they were fed and given iron to pump. They've watched you grow and subtly influenced the way you think about yourself. They've kept you where they want you by learning precisely when to strike and doing so with astonishing velocity and accuracy.

Bear in mind, as you work to create change and climb out of the hole they stand watch over, if they catch you off-guard, while you toil away, you don't stand a chance. Funny thing is, they've been wreaking havoc in your life probably for as long as you can remember - you've just grown accustomed to the carnage.

I previously mentioned the role the demons played in obscuring my life path.

Like Jack, they had me believing there were "acceptable" and "unacceptable" paths for me to travel down. Ultimately, after having trekked so many years down the one path deemed "best" I was unsure how to proceed in any other direction. Even considering veering from my tried-and-true, established course made me uncomfortable. It was this discomfort I closely examined to determine why I felt unable to deviate.

After all, how could I entertain different paths, if stepping off the well-worn one felt so scary? What had me so paralyzed?

Let me introduce you

Through my introspection, I discovered that there are four main players (like the Four Horsemen of the Apocalypse) that held me back. They operate in very similar ways for Jack and Marin, and when you look closely, you'll see how they have been operating in your head, too.

They are Impostor Syndrome, Invulnerability, and the twins, Risk and Failure Aversion.

Meet the Demons:
- *Impostor Syndrome*
- *Invulnerability*
- *Risk Aversion*
- *Failure Aversion*

With every opportunity, they loom large. With every success, they become more belligerent. They suck the joy out of every endeavor. They have guarded the hole and have become one with it. They are the dirt wall, the spider web, the ocean of ooze.

If you want to create your own fulfilling life path, you'll have to get through them first.

For starters, let's look at how they've manipulated poor Marin.

Demon #1: Impostor Syndrome

Impostor Syndrome goes straight for the self-esteem jugular. He tells Marin she's not good enough to be in the position she occupies, and that, soon enough, everyone will recognize she's a fraud and the charade will be over. She'll lose it all and go down in raging flames of embarrassment and humiliation. Impostor Syndrome makes her doubt her accomplishments and credentials at every turn. He holds a flashing neon sign that reminds Marin of her shortcomings, real and fabricated. Impostor Syndrome informs her that she may have everyone else fooled, but he knows the truth about who and what she really is.

Have you ever felt that way?

It seems to me, most folks have. My students certainly have. I work with freshmen in their very first semester at college. No matter how intelligent they are, each of them has a nagging concern that he or she doesn't really belong there. They worry everyone else in the classroom is better prepared to tackle college than they. Each of them seems convinced that at any moment someone is going to realize they're dumber than dirt.

For this reason, I start my classes out on the first day by asking students to put their heads down on their desks and raise their hand if they feel this concern. Almost every time we hit 100%. It is comforting for them, though, knowing they are not alone in this uncomfortable space.

So, perhaps it will comfort you to know you and Marin, and freshmen college students, and CEOs of Fortune 500 companies, and probably even Miss Universe contestants, all share this common insecurity.

Demon #2: Invulnerability

Invulnerability likes to trail close behind Impostor Syndrome. He says to Marin, "Stay strong, sister. Always do your best. But never, under any circumstance, let them see you cry or show weakness. Better stay on top and be the best in the bunch. Oh, and don't let anyone get too close, they might see the cracks in your foundation."

Marin believes, in her heart of hearts, Invulnerability is right. But Invulnerability is a damn creeper, too. He doesn't just show up in the light of day at her workplace. He sneaks into her house at night. When she tucks Christine into bed, he comes up real close behind her and whispers in her ear, "Don't tell anyone you're concerned about Christine saying she doesn't have a daddy. Don't let them know you're worried about making it on your own." Then he runs off giggling like a squirrely maniac while Marin's stomach churns.

I was on a first-name basis with Invulnerability for years. I'll bet you know this feeling, too, don't you? He's definitely the alpha-demon, so you're going to spend a significant amount of time analyzing and turning the tables on Invulnerability. In the meantime, if you have a dart board at home, draw this dude a face and stick it right onto the bullseye.

Demons #3 and #4: Risk and Failure Aversion

Risk and Failure Aversion operate in tandem most of the time and they love to swoop in when Invulnerability has Marin feeling weak. But, even at her proudest moments, they're there to kill her buzz.

Take, for instance, the time Marin's boss bragged on her performance in a meeting. Marin felt so great, she considered sharing with him her observation about a potential way to streamline operations and save the firm some cash. But Risk Aversion saw the spark in Marin's eye and doused it quickly with a bucket of ice-water. "Leave well enough alone, little lady. You might be wrong," he told her. "Or your boss could get mad at you for pointing out something he should have caught," Risk Aversion added.

So, Marin did nothing.

Failure Aversion is the real joker here, though. He'll distract Risk Aversion when he can and let Marin make an assertion or share an idea. Then, when her boss says, "Thanks, Marin, we'll take that into consideration." Failure Aversion laughs at her. He then grabs a bullhorn to beckon Impostor Syndrome, Invulnerability, and Risk Aversion back to the main line. Failure Aversion screams into the bullhorn, "Marin took a risk! And look at her now! They're 'taking it into consideration.' HA HA HA HA HA HA HA! That's code for 'you're so stupid we can hardly stand it. Let's return to our offices now and laugh and mock you'."

Stein

I know – harsh, right?

See how they've created conditions that make you feel safer, and more comfortable, just remaining in your hole?

They are going to be formidable adversaries. So, you need to study them. You need to learn how they operate. Perform your due diligence, get a handle on their MO, and prepare your artillery. This is no job for a pearl-handled .38 Special. You need to nuke these a-holes. Obliterate them and you'll be ready to forge ahead and lay the paving stones on your path.

It's the only way.

I'll wait while you do some crunches and chug a protein shake.

From this point on you're going to embark on a structured intervention. Some people might see it as guided therapy. Only you can decide how intensive you'd like this experience to be.

You might determine that a quick perusal of the remainder of this book and a sampling of the exercises is all you desire at this point. If you scored a 13 or above on each of the four dimensions of the PACT, perhaps an overview is all you'll require to adopt a new progressive frame of mind.

On the other hand, if your scores were lower, you might want to follow the exercises to the letter to promote the most effective and lasting change. Of course, you can always just expend the level of effort you can muster at the moment and revisit these pages later.

Note how the chapters and exercises build upon one another. While you completed Part 1 relatively quickly, and now have a deeper understanding of the dynamics that brought you to this point, Part 2 focuses on personal insights and will involve deeper introspection through personal assessment and experimentation. Part 3 is where you will initiate significant life change. It's one thing to understand the need for and approach to creating personal change, but it's a whole new ball game to actually implement change.

If you decide not to follow the exercises to the letter, you will reap the greatest benefit if you skim the entirety, then decide on which chapters to focus your greatest attention. Be forewarned though, as is

46

the case in therapy, success with the advanced work typically requires execution of the foundational work. Do not become discouraged if it takes you a few weeks or months to work through all the parts of this book.

I'm going to proceed as I would in face-to-face psychotherapy and in the classroom, operating under the assumption that you're hanging on my every word and you intend to follow every directive to the best of your ability. (You *are* going to hang on my every word, aren't you?)

The reason I requested you sign a pact was because I know you'll get out of it what you put into it. I also know the exercises are demanding, but effective.

So, from here, it's up to you. But you've already come this far, why let the engines cool?

Huddle up, here's the game plan

Are you ready to develop a plan to get yourself out of your hole?

You're going to tackle Invulnerability first. He's the team captain. Without him, the others are significantly handicapped. Slay him and your emergence from the rut and destruction of the dirt wall will be much easier. So, your first task is... (drum roll, please):

Become Vulnerable

Aaaaaarrrrrggghhhhhhhhh!!!!!!!! Noooooooooooooooo!!!!!!!!

Done now? Don't worry. Everyone has that same reaction. You're going to do this in graduated steps. I'm not an advocate of ripping off the band-aid, so you'll proceed slowly. I promise.

You'll need to study Invulnerability's ways, learn how he tailors his approach specifically to your situation, and then begin to patiently and steadily dismantle his grip. Yeah, it's going to require some work on your part, but you're climbing out of a hole, for crying out loud. There was bound to be some effort involved.

Your first drill

To better understand Invulnerability's hold on you, let's examine a situation in which this particular demon would have you feeling especially uncomfortable. What would that situation involve? Talking in front of a crowd? Meeting an attractive member of the opposite sex? Going #2 in a public restroom? (I know, people have some strange hang-ups.)

When you think about a situation in which you would assuredly doubt yourself and become completely rattled, write that situation out on line 5. Now, think about how you could make that scenario just a little less threatening, and write it out on line 4. Do that again with lines 3, 2, and 1. Line 1 should resemble line 5, but involve a set of conditions that would not leave you feeling stressed.

By way of example, here's Marin's list:

1. Making a presentation in front of family and friends
2. Making a presentation in front of my work friends
3. Making a presentation in front of my employees
4. Making a presentation in front of my supervisors
5. Making a presentation in front of the entire C-suite

Your list:

1. _____
    _____
2. _____
    _____
3. _____
    _____
4. _____
    _____
5. _____
    _____

Think about the difference between the first thing on your list and the last. What makes them different? Why does Step 1 seem relatively innocuous while the thought of Step 5 makes you consider the potential benefits of retreat to a foreign land?

For Marin, the overarching concern is that she'll screw up the presentation in front of influential people. Maybe she'd sweat and her hands would shake, making her appear weak and/or gross. That's not too great a concern in front of her friends and family. It's not likely to happen in that situation; and even if it did, although they'd rib her, she knows they love her, sweaty pits and all. But what if she trips over her words or gets her facts wrong in front of the CEO? Then, her "inferior nature" that she tries so desperately to conceal, will be right there on display.

Thinking about engaging in the last step of Marin's vulnerability list brings to mind the Whack-a-Mole game. Marin envisions performing the last step as the equivalent of poking her head out of the mole-hole. And, when she thinks about doing that, she also imagines a great big hammer coming down on her, whacking her back into her hole. Invulnerability wields that hammer. If Marin ever wants to successfully climb out, she knows she's going to need to disarm him first.

Identify the cracks in your defenses

Invulnerability holds his ground, because, like any bully, he's got the bluff on you. He knows your secrets and how to push your buttons like nobody else. To get at Invulnerability, you're going to have to pinpoint these facets for yourself. You'll have to determine your own Achilles heel.

Look back at the last item on your list. What does it say about the thing you'd least want anyone to know about you?

If you can't immediately identify it, that's okay, but you've got to recognize this crack in your armor. This is the facet over which you fight, ironically, most ferociously to maintain Invulnerability. Until you identify it and strip it of its power to intimidate and control you, you will not be free to escape.

Perhaps, you need an additional prompt or a double-checking method to ensure you are identifying that aspect of your psyche you'd be most concerned about anyone else becoming privy to. Engage in a deeper exploration through the 5 Why's exercise.

The '5 Why's'

Let's figure out what's at the heart of your insecurity and need to maintain a stance of invulnerability by asking "Why?" about your step #5, five iterative times. Each response should serve as the prompt for the next question.

Like this:

1. <u>Marin</u>: Why would it be so terrible to give a presentation in front of the CEO?
    <u>Why</u>: Because I'll get nervous and sweaty and trip over my words.

    <u>Why would it be so terrible to ... (insert your step #5)</u>
    _____?
    <u>Because...</u>_____
    _____
    _____
    _____
    _____
    _____

2. <u>Marin</u>: Why would it be so terrible if you sweat and trip over your words?
    <u>Why</u>: Because it will be obvious how flustered I am.

    <u>Why would it be so terrible...</u>_____
    _____?
    <u>Because...</u>_____
    _____
    _____
    _____
    _____
    _____

3. <u>Marin</u>: Why would it be so terrible if they knew you were flustered?

   <u>Why</u>: Because they'd know I'm not confident and they'd be distracted from my message by my sweaty armpits.

   <u>Why would it be so terrible...</u>

   _____?

   <u>Because...</u> _____

   _____

   _____

   _____

   _____

4. <u>Marin</u>: Why would it be so terrible if they saw you as less than confident with sweaty pits?

   <u>Why</u>: Because they'd think I can't do the work

   <u>Why would it be so terrible...</u>

   _____?

   <u>Because...</u> _____

   _____

   _____

   _____

   _____

5. <u>Marin</u>: Why would it be so terrible if they questioned whether you could do the work?

   <u>Why</u>: Because they'd think I'm incompetent and don't belong in their company.

   <u>Why would it be so terrible...</u>

   _____?

Because..._____

_____

_____

_____

_____

BINGO! There you have it.

Marin is afraid of being seen as incompetent. That's understandable, though, isn't it? Everyone wants to be construed as competent.

But, here's the glitch... does she have control over other peoples' perceptions? Or, does she only have control over how she presents herself? Will her excessive concern over others viewing her as competent (something Marin can't completely control) undermine her ability to present herself as confident? Especially considering the way her anxiety makes her pits sweat? And, do we know for sure Marin is reading the situation and their responses accurately? (Answers: No, Yes, Yes, Yes, and No).

For a truly wonderful and entertaining overview of the role of vulnerability as a driver of behavior and mindset, check out Dr. Brené Brown's TED talk, "Listening to Shame."

Reviewing the scrimmage

Do you see a little more clearly now how Invulnerability has empowered himself? Can you see why confronting him means confronting those aspects of yourself you'd just as soon pretend didn't exist?

You've work hard to ensure no one recognizes the facets that make you uncomfortable. And, why do you have these defenses and feel unsettled? Because you have grown to compare yourself unfavorably to others (like Marin) or consider yourself on constant unsteady evaluative ground (like Jack).

Those are the means through which Invulnerability enlists Risk and Failure Aversion, calls in Impostor Syndrome for back-up, and comes to control you. In reminding you of the ways you've fallen short in the past and what you stand to lose if you let down your guard, he ensures you maintain the wall around the hole that provides his safety and security.

Your insecurities and the will to ensure no one finds out about them serve as the feeding trough of this mind demon. By continually playing his game, you nourish him and he remains strong enough to prevent you from exploring novel means of achieving fulfillment, thus ensuring you remain his caretaker, deeply ensconced in your hole.

Think about the times you've tried to climb out of your hole. What happened? Was it a scary experience?

Most of the time, simply contemplating peering out of the hole is frightening. The Whack-a-Mole hammer always seems to be hanging precariously above. Nonetheless, on those occasions when Invulnerability has allowed you a glimpse of sunlight and freedom, you likely formulated ways to capture the light. Then, back in your confining dark space, you hatched the plan that would set you free and you mustered the will to run for it. Emboldened, you crept out just enough to make sure the coast was clear. Just then, Risk and Failure Aversion freed the hammer to swing a hair's breadth from your heads, just to ensure you remembered the potential consequences. On such occasions, hearing Invulnerability cackling in the shadows, I'll bet your nerves were shot and you lost your gumption, retreating back into the confines of your hole.

Perhaps you're realizing the many ways Invulnerability has kept you from enjoying life and reaching your potential. Maybe you're right now thinking of all the times you sold yourself short or all the wonderful people you unnecessarily kept at bay. You might be getting a bit pissed off at Invulnerability. Maybe, you're ready to go right out and cut him off at the knees. Good! He's got it coming.

But remember, grasshopper, he's been honing his skills for a long time.

To create your new path, you must change your mindset. I'm guessing at this point you might be entertaining the notion of letting down your defenses a little. But, there's not much that terrifies most people more than emerging from the hole in a vulnerable state. Still, now you've achieved insight into the importance of vulnerability and the role it plays in promoting the process of learning.

How then, do you change your mind about opening yourself up and revealing your shortcomings and weaknesses?

You start by figuring out the game Invulnerability plays and reversing his psychology.

Analysis of the opponent's playbook

Let's review what you've learned about our demon opponents' strategies.

Invulnerability tells you that you have to be competent. He doesn't tell you how to become competent, only that it's always expected that you will be competent. How tricky is this? Essentially, he recognized that to become competent/strong one must engage in the process of active learning. But he keeps this vital bit of information to himself. This way, when you make such efforts, he can call you out. He says, "By asking questions or revealing your soft underbelly, you've demonstrated that you are indeed not strong and competent. If you were strong and competent, you would not express naive curiosity or ask questions."

BAM! Catch-22! He's got you!

The minute you admit any sort of weakness, you're deemed incompetent. Not only that, but he's convinced you that incompetence is bad. To be incompetent is to be a lesser person. Shameful, even. But if you don't accept incompetence as a natural state, or that you will always be compromised in some form, you'll never work to improve your lot and become certifiably stronger.

> *If you don't accept incompetence as a natural state, you'll never work to improve your lot and become certifiably stronger.*

This goes right back to the "fixed" vs. "growth" mindsets and the development of grit.

Objectively speaking, though, it is a brilliant strategy, isn't it?

Did you catch how Invulnerability also conspires with Risk and Failure Aversion?

In Marin's case, they knew she wouldn't do anything that would make her feel or appear weak or incapable like consulting with the executives for clarification ahead of her presentation. To do so would amount to taking a risk and potentially standing out like a sore thumb among all the other people the demons have her convinced are competent in all the ways they've convinced Marin she is not. These demons will tell you repeatedly that should you take a risk, you *will* be called out when you fail. Risk and Failure Aversion use this to their advantage and run the same play repeatedly, knowing you'll fall for it almost every time.

These bullies have stacked the game in their favor. They've created conditions that ensure you'll carry on, focused on meeting external expectations, while denying your strengths and desires – and continually ignoring your blind spots.

Maybe at some point you managed to sneak in a triumphant play – one that totally caught them off-guard. Demon bullies breathe fire when they see us reap rewards. So eventually, lest you achieve a foothold, they invite the remaining goon, Impostor Syndrome, into the hole, and then leave you two alone, to become better acquainted.

Impostor Syndrome makes sure you know that he knows that while everyone else might think you have your head above the hole, and your act together, you're really only one misplaced foothold away from tumbling back into the depths of the abyss.

And as if that's not intimidating enough, guess what? Impostor Syndrome has one more trick play up his sleeve. The longer you allow the mind demons' intimidation to continue, and the more responsibility you assume in an effort to prove yourself competent, strong, and worthy, the more dominant Impostor Syndrome becomes. Eventually, you're left focusing solely on not making mistakes, almost like walking a tightrope – constantly concerned that the next step will be the false one that results in everyone realizing you are a phony, a sham, a fraud.

It's as though we live our lives in the shadow of the oversized Whack-a-Mole hammer. But it's not just you and me. You'd probably be amazed at how many physicians, therapists, and supermoms are emotionally crippled by the thought of being "found out."

Now you understand why Marin used to sweat when she had to deliver a presentation to a crowd of important people. No matter her level of preparation, she never felt as prepared as she should have been.

Invulnerability had ensured Marin didn't ask all the questions and learn everything she possibly could have through meeting with her bosses ahead of time for guidance. To do so would have, in her view, amounted to broadcasting the ways in which she didn't really warrant their esteem and confidence. In addition, he demanded Marin be poised and confident, all while repeatedly calling attention to the areas in which she was falling short. And even if she had performed impeccably, he'd still have told her it wasn't enough. The jerk.

Then Impostor Syndrome reminded her that even if she fooled the big boss, it was just one more card stacked on top of the precarious house she was building (which rendered Marin feeling even more anxious).

Subsequently, getting up in front of important people was fraught with risk. As she dwelled on the potential collapse of her carefully constructed house of cards, the probability of humiliation and failure (which her rapidly beating heart and clammy hands drove her toward) became more pronounced. Naturally, she then stumbled over her words and became increasingly conscious of her profuse sweating. Inevitably, Marin left each presentation convinced of her failure and focused solely on her shortcomings.

So, the demon bullies won every time.

Preparing for the next battle

I hope you see now why your first advance in this battle is to slay Invulnerability by refusing to accept his irrational premises. Once you accept his assertions at face value, the snowball begins its downhill descent.

~~~~~~~~~~~~~~~~~~~~~

CAUTION: Although you may be right with yourself in your own head, Invulnerability can be interpersonally transmitted like an STD. When you take ownership of your learning process and begin to ask questions, other peoples' demon spies might try to infect you with their Invulnerability, making you feel self-conscious that yours is showing. (Remember how you glared at Judy from Accounting when she asked questions?)

Have no fear!

You can put on protective armor and switch on your X-ray vision and see right through their ploy. However, without seeing clearly, the mind demons will ensure you interpret their looks and comments as darts and arrows preventing you from emerging from the hole.

With practice, you will realize their barbs are recognition of your courage and maybe even a little jealousy. This realization will fortify you. You will grow stronger with every inquiry. And, the coolest part is that you become Vulnerable Man/Woman by doing the exact thing

Invulnerability has been scared you would do and has gone to great lengths to prevent you from doing all along.

~~~~~~~~~~~~~~~~~~~~

You'd best start practicing your celebration dance.

 From here...

With an understanding of the opponents, a mindset open to exploration and opportunity, and unencumbered by defensiveness, you can investigate all manner of exciting possibilities. With your shoes off, your comfy pillow, a hot beverage, and your pen in hand, you are ready to take steps to climb out of the pit.

Eventually, you will need to put your shoes back on and begin paving the path. But, for now, take a bathroom break and allow me to share with you where my journey originated.

CHAPTER 4 TRAIL MARKERS

The demons keeping you sequestered in your hole are: Invulnerability, Impostor Syndrome, and the twins, Risk and Failure Aversion.

The demons ensure you remain focused on meeting external expectations.

Invulnerability doesn't tell you how to become competent, only that you're expected to be competent.

The more responsibility you assume to prove yourself a competent human being, the more dominant Impostor Syndrome becomes.

CAUTION: Other people may not be comfortable with your vulnerability.

CHAPTER 5

I told you, I get it

I'D LIKE TO SHARE with you my journey toward insight and the epiphanies I experienced while working to understand how I dug my hole, how the demons came to guard it, and what I had to do to climb out and forge a new fulfilling life path. If you are not in the least bit interested, or you're anxious to maintain your momentum, feel free to jump ahead.

I felt defeated

On September 4th, 2014, I wrote an email to a stranger. I'd seen his TEDx talk and he seemed like someone who might understand. While I'd suffered no specific trauma, my angst was palpable.

Ever since I was five years old, I wanted to be a psychologist. Odd dream, perhaps, but I have an uncle who is a psychologist and worked in an animal lab when I was very young. As a lover of animals, I thought it was the most interesting work anyone could do.

As my appreciation for psychology evolved over time, so did my area of focus; however, my interest never waned. Through graduate school, post-doctoral fellowship, private practice, research, and academia, I loved what I did and wound my self-concept intricately around my work. I was proud to be a Professor of Clinical Pediatric Health Psychology. I was proud of my PhD, and I was not at all put off by the ostentatious sound of my title. To the contrary, I was quite pleased with it.

At the time of my desperate email, I had spent fifteen years in the classroom, and had begun struggling to find meaning in my work. I had taken on numerous university leadership and committee roles and introduced new protocols into my classes in attempts to recapture my drive. But it all seemed futile. The connection was gone.

Despite being a wife, mother, daughter, friend, blah, blah, blah... it was my performance in the classroom by which I defined myself. At this point I was left wondering whether I'd ever provided anything of true value to my students and my university, and whether I ever would.

Hence, I questioned my reason for being, and to some extent, my value as a human being. I thought, maybe if I just try harder to make this happen... It had not occurred to me that perhaps I was furiously and blindly digging my hole, while failing to ask the questions that would have guided me out of the encroaching darkness

The subject line of the email I sent read: "Help! I'm suffocating here."

I could think of no other way to describe the experience of going in to the classroom every day. Previously, teaching had energized me. If I was having a dreadful day, I could go to class and, for fifty minutes I would be transported to someplace better. For fifteen years, the status quo provided me with fulfillment and made me feel important. But in the year leading up to my email, I felt as though each time I entered the room, I entered a vacuum. The moment I crossed the threshold, the air was sucked out of the room. My movements and lectures felt robotic. I was stuck feeling detached and depersonalized.

I wrote to Dr. David Helfand because he had experienced travails at Columbia University and at the time, was serving as President of a newly formed experimental university called Quest, in Canada. I thought David might relate to my struggles and share some words of wisdom about how best to resolve my funk.

To my surprise, he wrote back almost immediately. He recognized my pain and reached out to me to commiserate. We spoke at length about the frustrating administrative architecture of universities, apathetic students, workload demands, and creative pedagogical paradigms. It helped a bit.

> *Dr. David Helfand, is a Renaissance man and a revolutionary. His TEDx talk, "Designing a university for the new millennium" helped me begin to realize something major was missing from my life. David helped me identify the missing pieces and conceptualize ways to approach the challenge before me.*

David subsequently invited me to visit him at Quest University. This visit proved to be a turning point for me. I left with innovative ideas and a shift in my teaching philosophy.

My previous path... toward destruction

A few life events in the years prior to my visit to Quest precipitated my mid-life crisis.

First, my son, my elder child, was looking at universities. He had decided to study software engineering (I'm still convinced he chose this discipline because I am a technophobe and knew absolutely nothing about the field, and therefore couldn't nag him about it), so I delved into articles and blogs to read about the "soft skills" companies look for when hiring. I wanted to ensure he received the sorts of experiences in college, outside of his classes, that would make him an attractive candidate upon graduation.

As I searched the internet, several factors consistently emerged. They involved the development of an innovative and creative mindset, an ability to work in teams, and communication skills. As I related all this to my son (jokes on him, I still found something to nag about!), it occurred to me that I wasn't delivering such experiences to my college students. With my enthusiasm renewed, I generated experiences to ensure my students became creative and innovative, while communicating to one another through pre-planned, semi-structured group activities.

Did that sound stilted to you? Because that's exactly how it felt when I implemented the activities outlined in the numerous books I was reading. Essentially, I was trying to forge a path while still stuck in my hole, believing I was seeing the world clearly. It was as though Failure Aversion outstretched his arms to hold Invulnerability, Impostor Syndrome, and Risk Aversion back, while saying, "No, no, no guys, just wait for it... (then he probably winked at them) Just watch and wait."

He knew me so well.

In March 2012, over Spring Break, my son and I embarked on the grand college tour. A couple days before we were scheduled to leave, I began hemorrhaging severely from my girly zone. I called my gynecologist, who suggested a change to my oral contraception regimen. This worked temporarily, providing the sense of relief I needed to ignore the fact that, the night before we were to depart, I stood up and passed out cold, banging my elbow and head as I dropped.

Nevertheless, I was strong, soldiered on, and we arrived the next day in Alabama.

While my son sat in a class, I had an administrative assistant take me to the ER, since the bleeding had returned and was extremely heavy, causing me difficulty in walking. The ER doc had me complete a pack of birth control pills in two days. Voila! No more bleeding for a day or so.

On to Boston we went, and I was feeling better.

Then, it started again. I didn't want to worry my son, but I couldn't sleep as I passed clots the size of beef livers in adult diapers. (TMI? Sorry.) Justin had to push me around in a wheelchair by the time we made it to Rochester, NY. Still, I was driving and could walk about fifty feet at a time. When I arrived home, I made another appointment with my gynecologist. He drew some of what was left of my blood, but wasn't terribly concerned, since I walked down the hall, slowly, for the draw. He called about an hour later, while I rested at home, to tell me to come to the hospital, ASAP. Seems I'd lost nearly 60% of my red blood cells and was in imminent danger of organ failure.

Lying in the hospital bed, receiving blood transfusions, I began the process of life review. I was on the downside to fifty, my son was going off to college, my work was unsatisfying, and I had come within a hair's breadth of grave bodily harm. Curiously, at the time, my overwhelming feeling was pride in having completed the college tour, despite the serious danger I put myself and my son in. Had I been aware at the time, I'd have noted this as a milestone on my path to existential crisis and self-destruction.

Bumping up against the wall

I tried in vain for a year after visiting David at Quest to foster a climate of creativity and innovation on my campus. Not being a particularly patient person, working in an institution reluctant to change further taxed my emotional reserves. Activities intended to promote group discussion and divergent thinking in my classes were hit and miss. My frustration and agitation deepened over my inability to create any sort of meaningful change.

Initially, in my mind, failure to promote a magical transformation in the classroom meant something was wrong with my students for failing to recognize my clearly superior teaching skills. I further blamed the administration on my campus for not creating a culture supportive of the climate I was attempting to create.

For a while, I was angry and indignant. All the effort for naught was really pissing me off. I mean, how is it no one said, "Risa, you are onto something new and really innovative. You must be one of the most cutting-edge faculty members ever! We should all follow your lead!"

I felt I knew what was best for my classroom, and even my campus. If everyone would just listen to ME, my school would become a better learning environment for EVERYONE!

You can probably hear the mind demons patting one another on the back and high-fiving over their excellent work.

Deep down, though, I knew it also reflected on me. What was wrong with me that I hadn't yet become the best and most beloved professor on campus? What the heck was going on? From the way I saw it, I was putting forth 110% effort and the blasted world wasn't operating fairly in providing me the accolades I so obviously deserved.

It wasn't entirely about recognition. I truly wanted to make a difference. I really wanted the students to have a unique beneficial learning experience. However, as I look back on that time, it is evident that this desire was guided by my demons, not my genuine values. I felt I did the requisite legwork in reading my books and developing a plan. I was ready to prove what I knew. I shouldn't have to deal with the aggravation of persuading other people or running experiments; I should just BE (crowned) The Best.

Whose voice does that sound like?

Clarifying my vision and climbing out of the hole

Finally, a few things happened at once.

For starters, I familiarized myself with Dr. Brené Brown's work. Within the first few pages of her incredible book, *Daring Greatly*, Dr. Brown discusses the proclivity of researchers and academics to maintain an emotional distance, a sense of detachment and aloofness. She stated that for us, being too close to others often meant calling into question our illustrious reputation and stature. Upon reading this, a bell went off in my head.

For all my professional life people have described me as intimidating. I used to shake my head in mock disbelief and protest that I was, in fact, the nicest, most approachable person I knew. But in all honesty, I wore that sense of intimidation as a badge of honor.

After reading *Daring Greatly*, I wondered, in a particularly raw moment, while crouched in the dark recesses of my hole and the demons napped, "Could it be the university, the administration, and the students were not at fault in causing my existential crisis? Could it be that my propensity to keep others at an arm's length may have set me up for emotional angst?" This thought shook me to my core. Was I going to have to open-up to others in order to emerge from this hole? Ack! That hurt my brain and made me shudder.

Nevertheless, a glimmer of hope shone through the darkness and reached my tear-filled eyes.

Once I could see a little more clearly, I realized that my process of recovery from existential crisis would require deep introspection. I had to examine the reasons for my crushing need for control and recognition. Overwhelmingly, this meant I needed to re-evaluate my presence in the classroom. And I had to set new expectations for myself, in relation to creating campus change. I eventually concluded that I wasn't going to be able to force anyone to bestow upon me the title of "Professor Extraordinaire." In fact, I might even have to release all notions of attaining such honors.

Then, I fixed a bowl of ice cream and had a little pity party.

The new enlightened path

After this epiphany, I felt as though the light hitting my eyes guided me to Oz. Like Dorothy in a strange new land, I'd have to adopt a new persona and play under a new set of rules. I could never reach the Emerald City operating as though I was still in Kansas. Just as Dorothy had to follow the yellow brick road, learning more about herself as she traveled, so would I need to follow a new path and remain open to new possibilities. Following a new path would also force me to look inside myself and learn from difficult lessons.

Through a process of self-analysis and reading in multiple domains, including leadership, creativity, and innovation, I began to identify my Tin Man, Scarecrow, and Cowardly Lion. I found them among TED speakers, mentors, and authors. Like Dorothy, along the way I also encountered witches and flying monkeys. The first one I recognized, thanks to Dr. Brown, was Invulnerability. I saw his skywriting, "SURRENDER RISA" across various domains in my life, but most clearly, in the classroom. He told me I had to give in to him and his rules. I had to remain the 'sage-on-the-stage' with the utmost authority in the classroom. Risk and Failure Aversion, in their creepy flying monkey suits and little hats, circled close behind.

To reduce my veneer of power amounted to the introduction of an entirely new persona. So, I let my hair out of the braids, donned some ruby slippers, and took baby steps.

Trusting in the process and the path, I introduced myself as Risa, rather than Dr. Stein. I allowed my students opportunities to determine class structure. And slowly, I adopted the philosophy that they should operate as teammates with me. It became my imperative to join with them and empower them to learn, rather than seeing them as opportunities to demonstrate my impressive stature (as deluded as that may sound).

The transformation was almost instantaneous. The entire climate of my classes began to change. Students joked around with me more, were increasingly conversant in class (in part because I was able to control my urges to interject 'more important' points) and seemed more invested in learning. The feedback loop this created spurred me to read more, ask questions of faculty I admired, and experiment in the classroom and in my life, in general. I also became increasingly open to seeking and hearing feedback from students about my approach.

In essence, I locked arms with my class as we skipped down the yellow brick road together. It was scary at times, but it's been a fun adventure, as well. Although, along the way I could almost swear I heard the faint voices of previous students hiding behind desks singing, "Ding, dong, the witch is dead..."

Defeating the demons

In all, once I challenged Invulnerability, I became less Risk averse and more accepting of Failure. I still haven't won Professor of the Year. But one of the things I'm most proud of now is my ability to model a learner's mindset for my students, and to live the approach espoused in this book in the classroom.

Over the last couple years, I have seen students blossom under this perspective, finding in their hearts their personal, rather than societally-dictated definitions of success. I've had students thank me, in more sincere tones than I ever experienced before, for helping them gain self-knowledge by thinking about life critically, creatively, and more meaningfully. Students have sought my council as they contemplate new paths for their lives and careers. I have watched as they re-assess their own personal views of vulnerability and adopt a more open and active role in learning, taking risks and seeing failure as a self-discovery strategy, rather than a personal shortcoming.

It is only after great reflection and a process of trial-and-error learning that I have slayed my demons and paved my path beyond the hole. Because of this reinvigoration, I have been able to promote true meaningful change in myself, in my classes, on my campus - and even with regard to opening doors and widening my horizons for the next phase of my life.

 From here...

In the following chapters I will outline the approach Jack, Marin, and I took to climb out of our holes and pave our fulfilling life paths. It involves engaging in the PACT you made.

If we can pull it off, I know in my heart-of-hearts, you can, too.

CHAPTER 6

Do you know where you're going to?

Do you know where you're going to?
Do you like the things that life is showing you?
Where are you going to?
Do you know?

Now looking back at all we've planned
We let so many dreams
Just slip through our hands
Why must we wait so long
Before we'll see
How sad the answers
To those questions can be[3]

BY NOW YOU'VE ESTABLISHED your commitment to become unstuck and to forge your own life path. In the event you've forgotten, return to your signed pact and read it aloud!

However, before you rush in, guns blazing, you need to get the lay of the land. So, let's consider where you've been, where you are

---

[3] Songwriters: Gerry Goffin / Michael Masser
Theme from Mahogany lyrics © Sony/ATV Music Publishing LLC

currently, and where you DON'T want to be in the future. This way you can set up some guideposts and figure out where to stop for a drink along the way.

Your goal in this chapter is to gain the level of insight into your hole-digging behavior and the aftermath necessary to create a personally-tailored fulfilling life path.

This will be a very thought-provoking chapter.

Your experiences have contributed to who you are and the choices you've made. For this reason, you need to engage in a deep exploration of both and consider the ways they've contributed to you becoming stuck in your hole. Then you can move along to strategizing how to get out.

From a strategic perspective, the work you engage in across the following pages is designed to address the *Process* of learning; the "P" in PACT. While you may strive to learn something new every day, often these learning experiences are external in nature. You might learn the meaning of an unfamiliar word, a new more efficient route to your favorite restaurant, or all about a super-duper supplement that will help you lose fifteen pounds in no time. Learning new things is wonderful. What's even better is when learning provides insights into aspects of yourself with which you may have lost touch.

The luxury of being stuck

Being stuck provides you an awesome learning opportunity. It's a luxury, really. Many people operate on autopilot their whole lives, never allowing themselves the opportunity for self-reflection. The poor souls dig their hole every day without ever realizing their lives could be so much more fulfilling.

But, you... YOU have arrived at your impasse. Hence, you have a golden ticket to recreate your life's journey. Woo hoo!

Yeah, I know... I didn't feel much like Woo hoo-ing as I was lying in that hospital bed, but this really is a significant life turning point. Take a moment to appreciate how momentous it truly is.

~~~~~~~~~~~~~~~~~~~~

I'd like to pause for a moment to issue a qualification. Most people experience some, maybe many, positive and reinforcing aspects of their current path that preclude them from completely changing course. Maybe your unfulfilling job finances your fabulous vacations. Or, perhaps, your unfulfilling relationship nevertheless provides the family stability you didn't have while growing up.

Despite enjoying facets of your path, often for a great long time, you can still feel stymied.

There are always reasons why you stay the course and reasons why you feel a sense of trepidation in forging a new path. You may decide later that your current path still aligns best with your superordinate values. I want you to know that's okay. You might also feel as though, due to a financial or family situation, for instance, that you can't entirely scrap your path and forge a completely new one. I get that, too.

In that event, I hope to at least help you develop the visual acuity you'll need when you step out of your hole, to take note of the rewarding vistas that surround you. Even if you don't stray far, seeing the scenery with fresh eyes can put a hop in your step and inspire a sense of awe.

Think of it this way, even if your only available drink is wine, you can still add some fruit and make it sangria!

~~~~~~~~~~~~~~~~~~~~

Moving right along...

When did you first note you were stuck in a hole? Were you slipping in slowly, over time? Or, did you instead wake one day staring up through the darkness in search of a glimmer of light?

I'd like you to think about the timeline and course of events, thoughts, and/or insights that signaled to you that you were, indeed, stuck.

Specifically, you'll want to examine the impact being holed up has had on your life. To do so, you're going to take a closer look at the three areas Diana Ross sung about: Past, present, and future. This might not be easy, but it's necessary.

With each response to the following exercise, you are gaining additional clarity. When you're done, you'll be closer to safe ground outside your hole. You will refer back to this exercise in future chapters, so when you've completed this section, please bookmark this page.

Begin with the PAST. *Consider everything – the physical, the emotional, the people, the opportunities... everything.*

1. What have you missed out on by creating and remaining mired in your hole?
    (Example: Backpacking across Europe before entering graduate school)

    _____
    _____
    _____
    _____
    _____

2. Of the things you've missed out on, what would you most like to reclaim?
    (Example: My flexibility to travel)
    a. _____
    _____
    b. _____
    _____
    c. _____
    _____

3. On a scale of 1 (not strong at all) to 10 (overwhelmingly strong), list and rate the emotions you feel as you reflect on the losses identified in #2.

Emotion	Rating (1-10)
(Example: Regret)	(8)
a. _____	_____
b. _____	_____
c. _____	_____

Now, think about the PRESENT. *Consider everything, again — the physical, the emotional, the people, the opportunities... everything.*

1. What have you sacrificed in the time you've spent stuck in the hole?

(Example: The possibility of a happy union with my spouse)

_____

_____

_____

_____

_____

_____

2. Of the things you have forgone or lost while stuck, what would you most like to reclaim?

(Example: The emotional intimacy I shared with my spouse)

a. _____

_____

b. _____

_____

c. _____

_____

3. On a scale of 1 (not strong at all) to 10 (overwhelmingly strong), list and rate the emotions you feel as you reflect on the sacrifices listed in #2.

Emotion	Rating (1-10)
(Example: Disappointment)	(9)
a. _____	_____
b. _____	_____
c. _____	_____

And, last, think about the FUTURE. *Once more, consider every-thing – the physical, the emotional, the people, the opportunities... everything.*

1. What will you likely miss out on if you remain in the hole?
(Example: Learning to pilot a plane)

_____

_____

_____

_____

_____

_____

2. Of the things you'll likely never have or experience, what would you most like to claim?
(Example: Reconnecting with my former best friend)

a. _____

_____

b. _____

_____

c. _____

_____

3. On a scale of 1 (not strong at all) to 10 (overwhelmingly strong), list and rate the emotions you feel as you reflect on the potential losses listed in #2.

Emotion	Rating (1-10)
(Example: Sadness)	(10)
a. _____	_____
b. _____	_____
c. _____	_____

Nice work. Set this book or your journal aside for a while and rest your brain.

Reflect on your journey

Take a moment to reflect on what you previously wrote. Is there anything, upon review you'd like to add or modify? If so, go ahead and do so.

To this point, you have simply characterized your experience of facing a life spent in the abyss. Although you've approached it in general terms, including why you ended up in this state, you've not addressed it on a personal level.

Take a moment to reread your responses to what you have missed out on so far and what you risk missing out on in your years to come if you remain stuck. Think intently about the experiences and opportunities you described.

Consider carefully your emotional responses to these sacrifices and losses. It's not uncommon to become increasingly emotional as you do so. That's okay. Really.

Get yourself a tissue and a bowl of ice cream. You're doing fabulous work.

I encourage you to bookmark the previous page with your past, present, and future losses. We'll revisit this section in a later chapter.
It is useful to have handy, the costs of remaining stuck in your rut.

Consider the amount of time you've spent stymied. How does this fit with the insights you gained about your vulnerability Achilles heel? Do you see the relationship between the fear Invulnerability instilled in you and the resulting losses you incurred? You can't reclaim lost time, but you can ensure the years ahead are the most fulfilling years possible.

You're going to revisit these insights, regrets, and wishes as you move through later chapters to the Active learning component and the Thoughtful application of learning. Some of the work I'm going to ask you to engage in may tax you a bit. Hence, it is useful to have in front you, in black and white, the costs of remaining stuck in your rut. It's too easy to become complacent during emotionally trying times and to revert to autopilot.

I don't want you to dwell on what you've lost, but I do want you to consider the forces that have been so powerful in your life that you have been propelled down a path that precluded you from attaining the experiences and opportunities, which you now regret missing.

If you have difficulty getting to the root of the cause, work through them by asking the "5 Why's" again. For example, when I think about why I made the decision to forgo backpacking through Europe when I was younger, I initially consider the financial barriers, the lack of travel companions, and my overall trepidation over navigating foreign lands. Certainly, these factors played a role, but they weren't insurmountable.

Upon deeper introspection, I come around to the realization that in large part I was in a hurry to earn my doctoral degree to prove my worth and show that I'm "better" than the kids who teased me in school. My path was paved by insecurity and spite. It colored the way I viewed the world, interacted with others, and shaped my future. It fast-tracked me down paths that bypassed some of the most interesting vistas available. Eventually, it diminished my vision in a way that limited my interactions with students and decreased my effectiveness and enjoyment of my work. That mindset and my need to avoid vulnerability nearly caused my demise. Sheesh! This is precisely why I describe facing a life impasse as a golden opportunity. It's the smack-in-the-face wake-up call so many people need before it's too late.

It's a relatively safe assumption that once you've drilled down to what got you and kept you in the hole, it will come back to fear of being perceived as incompetent, weak, or imperfect. It almost always boils down to our old nemesis, Invulnerability. Now, hopefully, you see it in a more personal and motivating way. Rightfully, you're also energized to vanquish Invulnerability and take advantage of the opportunity before you.

Therefore, our next empowering activity must be geared toward overcoming Invulnerability.

As I mentioned very early on, I had to learn to deal with him, and so will you. For me, establishing domain over Invulnerability meant tearing down the veneer of intimidation that protected my deepest irrational insecurity and allowing people to get to know me.

This was challenging after living nearly forty-years guided by a mindset created when I was eleven years old to defend against real life bullies. I felt that so long as I was accomplished and intimidating, I could keep people at arm's length and maintain appearances, while sparring with Impostor Syndrome, the internal menace echoing the taunting voices of my youth.

For Jack, it meant deviating from the safe path he allowed society to establish for him. Since Jack relied almost solely on guidance and reinforcement from others to establish his self-worth, he was also extremely Risk Avoidant, lest he make any move that could disappoint them and jeopardize what he experienced as conditional acceptance.

Marin, as we know, felt very unsure of herself. In her mind, she already had two strikes against her. Invulnerability conspired with Failure Aversion to lead her to practice such restraint over her actions that she sacrificed growth and happiness for a sense of stability.

From here...

To create a new mindset that will move you away from your hole, you need to overcome your fear of being vulnerable. Until you can acknowledge and conquer that, you cannot engage in the process of self-discovery and learning that paves a personally fulfilling path.

Early in my journey I tried to move forward in creating my own path under the condition that no one ever know of my insecurities. Invulnerability held a tight grip on my hand as he led me down the trail. Had I continued operating with that mindset, I likely wouldn't have attempted to write a book. And, if I had decided to write while guided by that perspective, there's no way I would have shared a rough draft with someone I admire, and no way in h-e-double-hockey-sticks that I would have detailed my fears in black and white (and sometime gross) detail. And, therefore, no way this journey could have been personally rewarding.

So, you need to leave Invulnerability at the nearest rest stop. He cannot make the journey with you. He holds on too tightly and eats all the chocolate chips from the trail mix.

CHAPTER 6 TRAIL MARKERS

Thoughtful learning puts you in touch with aspects of yourself you may have lost sight of.

You may still feel stymied despite enjoying facets of your current path.

Recognition of lost opportunities and time can reinforce your will to move forward.

Until you can acknowledge and conquer Invulnerability, you cannot engage in self-discovery.

CHAPTER 7

Tactical removal of mind demons

AT THIS POINT you may experience some mixed emotions. There might be sadness over lost time/relationships/opportunities, excitement over new possibilities, and trepidation over what lies ahead. That's all perfectly natural. In fact, you should view this as a very encouraging sign. It demonstrates your potential for vulnerability and readiness to move forward in forging your path.

There's no time to wallow in regret, though. You've got a fabulous life ahead of you to get to work on. So, let's not hesitate another moment and get right to work on shifting the mindset that steered you wrong.

It's time to get to work on pulling your hand from Invulnerability's tight grasp.

The next activity I'm going to ask you to try should challenge you a little. It involves spitting in the face of Invulnerability by demonstrating your capacity to do the opposite.

Recall that I began demonstrating vulnerability by asking my students to call me Risa. In my mind, that action made me approachable, which felt threatening to me. For Jack, the people pleaser, it involved planning a Saturday just for himself without concern for what anyone else would think of his plans, or whether they would be interested in joining him. Marin, who was overwhelmingly self-conscious, had a lower comfort level and started by wearing mismatched socks to work.

Oh, by the way, I know this process can be scary. Honestly, I understand. Invulnerability held you back all this time, but he also held your hand. You may feel a little exposed, uncomfortable, and alone while you complete these tasks. One way to lessen this anxiety is to invite a new friend to travel with you. A real flesh and blood human friend. In fact, telling a friend about the journey you are embarking upon and inviting them along for support is a really great way to start down your new path sans Invulnerability.

Throughout this chapter and the next few, you're going to accomplish several goals. It's important not to lose sight of your growth. To ensure you give yourself credit for all your hard work, you'll keep track. This practice also allows you to note the exciting adventures just around the bend. You'll probably catch yourself saying, "Next up is 'gaining comfort with the weak, imperfect, incompetent aspects of vulnerability'? Oh, yeah!! Now, I'm totally stoked!!"

~~~~~~~~~~~~~~~~~~~~

Here's the checklist you'll revisit after each endeavor to track your progress:

☐ gain comfort with the weak, imperfect, incompetent aspects of vulnerability
☐ expand your field of vision by trying something new
☐ develop and integrate your skill set
☐ align your skills with your values

~~~~~~~~~~~~~~~~~~~~

Removing the dirt wall

You'll start off slowly. Regardless, the suggestions I'm about to make might feel a tad overwhelming to you right now. Consider your comfort level, but also consider all the sacrifices you highlighted in the last chapter, and all you risk missing out on in the future if you don't push yourself beyond your Invulnerability-imposed comfort zone.

I'd like you to engage in activities from the list below or develop some of your own. Circle a few that seem well-suited for you. You know you've found a good one if, after reading it, you say, "Oh, heck no, I'm *never* doing that!" That's the one that's going to pull your hand out of Invulnerability's sticky grasp. That's the one that makes you an Active participant in the Process of learning about yourself.

Go ahead and try to vividly imagine engaging in the following acts. Note those that get the butterflies in your stomach fluttering.

- Ask someone to open an already loose jar for you
- Lift significantly less weight than is possible for you in front of others at the gym (extra credit for grunting loudly while doing so)
- Spill coffee in a meeting
- Trip up the stairs in front of others
- Drop food in your lap in a restaurant
- Complain about never being able to find your glasses/keys/water bottle (extra credit if they're in your hand)
- Ask for help with office equipment or machinery
- Ask a gas station attendant for directions
- Ask another grocery shopper what zucchini is and how to cook it
- Weep openly in a theater during a sad movie
- Buy three of the largest multi-packs of toilet paper rolls you can find
- Bring to work all the worst flavors of donuts
- Button your shirt wrong and keep it that way all day
- Leave the lipstick on your teeth
- Miss a noticeable patch of hair while shaving
- Moan perceptibly while using a public restroom
- Leave a small trail of toilet paper from the back of your pants
- Ask a stranger for a quarter
- Speak very loudly while ordering lunch

- Wear the princess tiara your daughter loves while out shopping with her
- Sing in your loudest voice with the windows down at the stop signs/lights
- Slurp your soup in public
- Fail to respond to anyone until they repeat themselves twice
- Read a book out loud in a public place
- Compliment a stranger
- _____
- _____

Were you able to find or design a few that will work for you? Good. Pick three activities that push you out of your vulnerability comfortzone. Repeat each twice around different people, if you can. Try to take notice of others' reactions. You needn't do them all on the same day. In fact, try to spread them out over the course of one-week, but no longer than a week, if possible. Set this book aside until you have completed this exercise. I'll hang back and hum the Jeopardy theme song until you're done...

Dirt wall removal review

How did it go?

If I may, I suspect a couple things might have happened. First, you were close to mortified going into it. If so, you may wish to ask yourself why you were mortified; although, by now I think we both know why (ahem, Invulnerability). Second, you expected everyone around you would make rude comments or stare at you and you would be completely humiliated.

After completing the activities, however, you probably experienced one or all of the following new realizations:

Either no one noticed your act at all. Nobody. Nada. None. And you realized you are not the center of the universe, because people are far more self-involved than you had previously appreciated.

Or, more people than you expected took note and maybe even said something to you about the act. In that case, you've likely reached the conclusion that some folks will upset themselves over very trivial things, or good people still exist and are kind enough to discretely let you know you have lipstick on your teeth.

Sometimes, the most interesting thing of all happens, though: You realize that being vulnerable and imperfect, at least when done intentionally, can be a whole lot of fun!

If you recall, Invulnerability operates on two basic assumptions. First, Invulnerability says that you must never appear vulnerable. You must always be competent, strong, and perfect, even though the only route to becoming so involves the demonstration of vulnerability. Second, he says that if you prove yourself vulnerable, you will appear weak, incompetent, and imperfect, and people will scorn you, and you will be humiliated and want to crawl right back into your hole.

You have just proven his equation false. You exhibited vulnerability on several occasions and you did not die from it. Even if you were embarrassed, you survived! In fact, you may have actually enjoyed it! Moreover, in the midst of your incompetence or weakness, rather than chastising or belittling you, you likely found people are genuinely caring and helpful. Yay, you!!!! You've stepped out of your hole and eluded the Whack-a-Mole hammer.

So, now that you know you can survive simple vulnerability, let's become more strategic about building competence. To help you plow through the wall of dirt around your hole, you'll need to gear your vulnerability toward the practice of exploratory learning and self-discovery. Don't fret, you'll take it a step at a time.

Just a minute...

Pause for a moment here to consider what you have accomplished.
Do you realize you have done something for yourself you might not have done since early childhood? Do you see that you've now climbed entirely out of the hole?
I think this is worthy of some sort of celebration. When was the last time you celebrated you?
Well, you deserve it!!
Treat yourself to a frou-frou coffee drink or a manicure or tickets to a ball game.
You've earned it!

~~~~~~~~~~~~~~~~~~~~

Let's keep track of your good work. Go ahead and put a big ol' check mark in the first box.

☐ gain comfort with the weak, imperfect, incompetent aspects of vulnerability
☐ expand your field of vision by trying something new
☐ develop and integrate your skill set
☐ align your skills with your values

~~~~~~~~~~~~~~~~~~~~

Keep it going

By engaging in the previous exercise, you totally destroyed Invulnerability's assumptions! You proved that you can demonstrate weakness, incompetence, and imperfection, and survive and even have fun with it. You've taken the first step and boosted your self-confidence. Now, you're out of the hole and ready to destroy the dirt impasse. You are prepared to conquer Invulnerability once and for all, by leveraging your capacity to demonstrate vulnerability in a purpose-driven fashion.

Your goal now moves from *exposure to vulnerability* to *strategic vulnerability*.

You're going to turn your attention to practicing vulnerability in the various facets of life that will benefit you most.

Gaining additional insight into who you are enables you to begin conceptualizing a path tailored to your desires. In doing so, you short-circuit the potential of becoming overwhelmed by a wide-open horizon, once the dirt wall comes tumbling down. In other words, it's time to Actively engage in the Process of learning about yourself. This step is going to move you into the realm of Curiosity, as well.

You've previously identified the people and activities you recognize having missed out on while digging your hole. And your life may indeed be more fulfilling if you work toward including them on your new path. But what of the adventures that never even made it onto your radar screen? Or those things you used to enjoy that have long ago fallen by the wayside and been forgotten? What about life's simple pleasures? All too often, the hole is a dark depressing place devoid of the simple pleasures that bring joy to existence.

To create a fulfilling life path, you need to embark on strategic and focused exploration. To do this, I've outlined four different areas in which people often find their views constricted. Once you push these boundaries, your field of vision becomes increasingly enriched, helping you achieve greater focus and purpose.

Novel activity exploration

Turn your attention now to widening your field of vision through strategic vulnerability. To do so, over the course of the next four weeks, engage in two novel activities per week, for a total of eight small, thoughtful learning experiments.

These activities will fall into the following categories: a) altering a habit or routine behavior, b) doing something you've wanted to do and haven't gotten around to, c) reclaiming something you used to do, but haven't done in a while, and d) "joie de vivre."

Here are some examples of such tasks:

Habit altering:

- Order lemon chicken rather than my usual orange chicken at the Chinese restaurant
- Go the opposite way on my walking route around my neighborhood
- Spend a few hours without my cellphone
- Hit the gym before work rather than after
- Part my hair on the left side instead of the right
- _____
- _____

    Reflection: _____

_____

Trying something new:

- Dye a temporary streak of purple color in my hair
- Make a new meal from scratch
- Go to a meet-up of people who share my interest in stamp collecting
- Practice mindful meditation
- Volunteer at an animal shelter
- _____
- _____

    Reflection: _____

_____

Reclaiming something you used to do:

- Play with kid's toys (Legos, Play-do, Silly Putty)
- Write poetry
- Take nature photographs
- Write an old-fashioned letter to an old friend

- Peruse the vintage clothing stores
- _____
- _____

  Reflection: _____

  _____

Joie de vivre:

- Play in the rain
- Collect wildflowers
- Slurp spaghetti
- Drink the milk from the cereal bowl
- Lay on the grass in my back yard at night and contemplate the stars
- _____
- _____

  Reflection: _____

  _____

You'll note that every category has two blank lines. These blank lines are there for you to add your personalized activities. Go ahead and write your ideas on those lines. If you can only think of a couple right now, that's okay. It may take some practice before your brain relaxes enough to get into the swing of it. Feel free to write down any subsequent ideas for each category as they come to you.

Remember, too, that when someone asks you to join them on an outing you might have automatically answered "no" to, while stuck in the hole or behind the dirt wall, you can go ahead and reply that you'd love to and write it down as one of your eight small experiments.

Remain as observant and curious as a three-year-old as you engage in these activities. With each activity accomplished, your field of vision and self-knowledge will expand. Reflect on these insights on the last line of each section. What did you experience anew or take note of for the first time or see in a completely different light?

You might wind up requiring additional activity or reflection lines. If you're not writing in a journal, feel free to write in the margins of this book. You are, after all, venturing outside of the lines here.

Engaging in these sorts of activities shakes up your normal existence. It forces you to view the world with fresh eyes. Many of them will also relax you out of your everyday stress. When you see the world differently by trying new things, your mind goes into a new gear, your eyes grow wider, and your taste buds are alerted. Not only that, your brains get excited and start thinking about other new things that might be cool and fun to try. Your brain might say, "OMG! Lemon chicken is so awesome! You know what, let's try sushi next!" And you'll try sushi. You might hate sushi but look at you go! You're trying new things, learning more about yourself, and taking additional steps down your new path with eyes wide open.

~~~~~~~~~~~~~~~~~~~~

Now you're rolling!! Once you've fulfilled your mission of trying new things, check off box #2 on the new path progress checklist.

- ▣ gain comfort with the weak, imperfect, incompetent aspects of vulnerability
- ☐ expand your field of vision by trying something new
- ☐ develop and integrate your skill set
- ☐ align your skills with your values

~~~~~~~~~~~~~~~~~~~~

How do you feel? Can you envision the barriers around the hole and your mind receding? Are you feeling increasingly liberated? I sure hope so! Feels super fantastic, doesn't it?

If you've not yet reached that point, I would suggest revisiting the past/present/future exercise. Is there anything you'd like to add? Anything you held back? How about the vulnerability exercise? Did you take a safe route? Did you choose activities that avoided butterflies?

It's tough sometimes, the first time around. If you haven't completely emerged from the hole and kicked at the dirt wall, cut yourself some slack. Some of us are a-toe-at-a-time-into-the-pool kind of folks. In fact, I imagine more of these folks are holding this book in their hands right now than head-first-into-the-deep-end folks. Take your time. There is no hurry.

But I cannot emphasize strongly enough how imperative it is that you focus intently on putting forth an honest effort to understand the means through which your circumstance was created. Superficial introspection is the equivalent of striking the dirt wall with a whiffle ball bat. Deep introspection, on the other hand, provides you a sledgehammer. You needn't rush your swings, but when you are ready, you ought not waste your time and effort.

Regardless of how you currently feel, by no means should you stop trying and doing new things. Just like practicing vulnerability, eventually you'll find that trying new things gives you a bit of a rush.

While you won't enjoy all your experiments, you'll find yourself learning about facets of your being you didn't know existed. This is because these activities nurture your Curiosity through Thoughtful and personalized experimentation. Engaging in small experiments allows you to realize and create a larger catalog of things you like and don't like.

This is the crux of the PACT. You are engaging in the Process of learning about yourself through Actively deploying Curiosity to create personally meaningful and Thoughtful experiments that reveal insights, opportunities, and new vistas. Good for you! With each new experiment, you are learning more about yourself and amassing tools to create a personally tailored and fulfilling life path, replete with an abundance of scenic vistas. Think of the insights as new Velcro hooks and loops in understanding and learning about YOU!

From here...

Let's keep the momentum going. Your mind is open. Your spirit is willing. You are far more comfortable now with vulnerability and are enjoying trying new things and learning more about yourself. You are well underway to clearing a route for your path.

Continue to remove the accumulated dirt and diminish the power the mind demons have over you by increasing your comfort in trying new things. The goal is to decrease your need for Invulnerability, but you may not have noticed, you are simultaneously diminishing your Risk and Failure Aversion. So, keep it up!

Let's move along to box #3, 'Develop and integrate your skill set', and see how you can more thoughtfully apply your newfound insights to open doors to additional opportunities. This is a big step. You're moving now into conceptualizing the new path.

Before you lay down the first paving stones, though, you have to get the lay of the land before you.

CHAPTER 7 TRAIL MARKERS

Invulnerability sends two messages: 1) You must never appear weak, incompetent, and imperfect, and 2) If you do people will scorn and humiliate you.

By practicing vulnerability, you prove Invulnerability's tenets FALSE!

Engaging in novel activities shakes up your normal existence and provides you with new perspectives on the world.

With each new experiment you learn more about yourself.

PART 3

PAVING YOUR PATH

CHAPTER 8

We're all flower children

AS YOU CLIMB from your hole and clear the dirt wall that blocked your vision through the implementation of curiosity-driven thoughtful experiments, you will discover facets of yourself that might have been hidden for years, or never even previously identified. I mean, how is it possible that you simply forgot how relaxing and enjoyable coloring can be?

These are crucial insights to integrate into your approach to paving a new life path. The more of your true being you can infuse into your existence, the more fulfilling your existence becomes. Frequently, folks struggling with moving forward in their lives describe a sense of disconnect and lack of integration. Keeping track of what you enjoy and find fulfilling will help you when the time comes to put all the pieces together.

Cataloging your likes and dislikes, and maintaining a list of experiments to run, might have you feeling like a kid in a candy shop. In fact, it's not unusual to want to just take some time and indulge yourself. I say, go for it!

But, keep track of your insights. Otherwise, it's human nature to forget about them when something new and shiny catches your attention. For this reason, I suggest keeping a running list of things you like and don't want to lose sight of. If you are maintaining a journal, put a sticky tab a few pages from the end and begin your catalog on that page. This way, you retain plenty of room to capture the experiences you've enjoyed, but it won't intrude on the flow of your exercises and development.

My list of things not to forget I enjoy:

(Example: Walking in the rain on a spring day, archery, slurping jello)

The next step in creating a path tailored to you, is putting all the activities you enjoy together with all the other activities in which you engage, to develop new insights. This is a very behavior-oriented approach. The thought behind focusing so heavily on your activities is that what you do impacts how you feel about yourself and vice versa. Ensuring that you engage in activities that adequately represent your true self is key to feeling fulfilled. It's pretty simple, really. Do what you enjoy, and you feel satisfied and happy. Completely neglect what you enjoy and what brings you satisfaction, and you feel unfulfilled – suffocated, even.

Visualizing an integrated picture of you

I like to have things in black and white in front of me. In fact, I think most people are rather visual and can see the relevance of small details much more clearly once the big picture is laid out before them.

In moving forward, you can fortify yourself through recognizing untapped personal resources. Furthermore, determining which activities sustain you and which drain you is important in establishing your new fulfilling path. To that end, this chapter amounts to your taking the first step in constructing the big, beautiful, integrated picture of YOU!

You are not a salad bar

Most people compartmentalize their lives into discrete units.

I'm a mother who engages in grocery shopping, cooking, and scheduling for my family. When I try a new recipe, the outcome typically remains within the realm of family. I'm also a professor who reads books, prepares classes, and serves my university through committee work. The knowledge I gain through reading innovation and creativity books is generally applied exclusively in my psychology classes.

And finally, I'm an individual who loves dogs, gardening, and travel. In the scheme of things, those aspects don't seem to fit well anywhere other than a seemingly useless "miscellaneous" category.

You might describe yourself in a similar fashion. However, relating myself as I just did makes me feel like I'm comprised of separate sectioned-off and compartmentalized bins on a salad bar. In fact, prior to crafting my fulfilling life path, in retrospect it often seemed as though I viewed my life as one might view the offerings at a salad bar. I proceeded through life partaking in one item from a bin at a time followed by a shot of ranch dressing. That's not a real salad and it wasn't a life benefitting from the integration of meaningful and enjoyable parts, either.

Your life should not be lived one item at a time. All of you is interesting! However, without such interconnectedness, it's easy to feel an overall sense of disconnect and eventually lose interest in your life. You end up feeling like you're playing a role in each domain, rather than feeling your true self is infused into everything you do.

Have you felt that way? The way Jack did – like you are playing a part in someone else's crappy B-movie? The key to reversing this is figuring out who you are and ensuring that who you genuinely are makes it into every scene played out in your life.

What you're going to shoot for in this chapter is integrating the various facets of your life. To begin conceptualizing just how many potential variations on your life there are, let's lay it all out in a way that facilitates interconnectedness.

Why draw a flower diagram?

The world of business and innovation often speaks of "T-shaped" people. The vertical base "l" represents one's depth of knowledge and the horizontal top line " ⁻ " represents breadth of knowledge and skills.

This is fine, but for me, it doesn't offer the visual I need to be able to note potential synergies between various skills, interests, and facets of my existence. The "T" is just one long line of salad bar offerings, often still pertaining only to one facet of an individual's life. For this reason, I prefer to use a flower diagram, such as this:

Rather than simply placing my various interests on a plane, I find it far more useful to wrap the line around in a way that visually enables less obvious connections.

Imagine you are standing in the middle of the flower, surrounded by the petals. Now, imagine the petals are salad bar bins. Isn't it easier to conceive of creating a fabulous salad with this perspective, rather than looking down a lengthy line of bins? Why sludge your way to the end, filling your plates to overflow with the least appealing front-end bulk items, while reserving precious little room for the appetizing toppings relegated to the end of the line? How do you even know what's down there? Why aren't real salad bars set up this way?

I'll have a talk with management about this.

Anyway, this is akin to what you previously saw taking place with our gingerbread house builders. Jennifer, who had limited knowledge in numerous areas, was able to combine her various skill sets and leverage each to build a most stupendous gingerbread house.

The others relied on their unidimensional skill sets without ever incorporating knowledge from various domains, and they wound up with inferior houses. You don't want another single-focus inferior life path, do you? NO! You want an integrated multifaceted life path that incorporates the various elements of your being and the activities you enjoy. Furthermore, you don't want an airtight tunnel of a path, you want one that allows the sunshine in and leaves room to incorporate all the new things you're finding out about yourself every day.

Drawing the picture of YOU

Let's begin by creating your flower diagram. Start with leaves constituting the primary hats you wear and a thick stem that is you. The petals would include all your interests and the tasks involved in the roles you play.

If your struggle is isolated to one aspect of your life, you can create a stem focused on that facet and begin with petals more pertinent to that area.

A high school graduate considering which college and career path best suits her, might draw a flower focused on her role as a student. "Student" would serve as the stem, and the largest petals would represent her student-related interests and skills: playing the clarinet, advanced math classes, volunteer work in teaching English as a second language. She can then elaborate and broaden her scope by adding petals for things she really enjoys, like creating YouTube make-up tutorials, designing prom dresses, and walking in the woods after it rains.

The flower diagram enables her to make her student-related activities front-and-center, without losing sight of everything else that makes her unique. It also allows her to see each aspect of her being in relation to the others, rather than segmenting her life and interests. This schematic facilitates creative pairings of discordant options, providing insights into which college or career path best fits her true being.

I can only assume this is also how pineapple and ham made it together onto the first Hawaiian pizza.

When I engaged in this exercise, I began with the area in which I felt most stuck – my academic work. I allowed the stem to represent my disciplinary work in clinical psychology. The leaves reflected the other primary roles I play. The petals represented all the areas involved in my job including committee work, research, student organization advising, and the areas I am interested in, innovation and creativity, nutrition, application of psychology in business, and interdisciplinary collaboration. This comprised the basic flower structure for my work.

Next, I included my home life by adding petals representing the additional activities associated with my spouse, mother, daughter, and friend roles. Other petals represented my household responsibilities along with the things I enjoy, such as dogs, travel, and gardening.

Through the construction of your flower diagram, you are essentially engaging in an inventory of who you are, without artificial, socially-imposed, subdivisions.

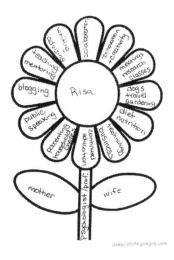

Our graduating high school student may have been considering a career in accounting, given her mathematical acumen and preference for alone time. Yet maybe this decision left her with an inexplicable, less-than-enthusiastic feeling. Without juxtaposing her mathematical abilities with her You-Tube tutorial and prom dress design interests, she may not have recognized alternatives or achieved insight into other potential options.

Once her flower diagram is completed, her mind might be open to other possibilities, such as architectural or interior design at a college in Florida or Seattle, where she can also experience the sense of renewal she enjoys while walking in nature after a long rain. Without such realizations, she may have inadvertently dug herself into a hole that ultimately left her feeling unfulfilled.

Completing your flower diagram moves you a step away from your hole and the grand dirt wall.

Still, a wide-open horizon can seem daunting. Creating your flower is akin to placing pushpins on a map. It enables you to begin formulating a path designed around the points of greatest interest to you, while also ensuring the route provides adequate room for exploration of additional worthwhile venues. Essentially, the insights gained through creating your flower provide guidance, like trail markers, that steer you toward areas of exploration consistent with the PACT. This makes the great wide-open a little less intimidating.

If you'd like you can take some time to color in the petals, add a big yellow sun and some grass, and relax a while.

Go ahead and complete your flower diagram in as much detail as possible. Make sure you have included activities you enjoy, and not just the roles you play or the tasks assigned to you.

Remember, it's often the toppings that add real verve to your salad. The same should hold true for your flower and your life. Move beyond an iceberg lettuce, tomato slices, and cucumber life. Go crazy! Add slivered almonds, dried cranberries, AND bacon bits!!

If you have a bud of a flower

There are folks, and you may be one of them, who find their flower has relatively few petals.

Marin found herself in this situation. I'll talk more about the steps she took to address this challenge in the next chapter.

In the meantime, if looking at your flower leaves you feeling depressed or full of regret, do not despair! Remember, this insight is a positive thing. You have identified at least part of the cause for the lack of fulfillment you feel. This is absolutely great news. It will be even better when you capitalize on this information to create positive change.

So, for now, if your flower is lacking, add petals for the things you've recently recognized you've missed out on or discovered you enjoy. Let's call these *"desire"* petals. They might pertain to activities you've identified in your past/present/future exercise, through your strategic vulnerability experiments, or something completely different that you've only recently realized you'd like to explore further. Go ahead and add these petals to your flower. Oh, and if you have a glitter pen, feel free to make these petals sparkle!

Putting your picture on display

An ideal next step involves harnessing your vulnerability power again. It seems unfair to humanity to keep your beautiful life picture to yourself. You deserve a gilded frame and a spot in the finest museum. I know, you're thinking you might not even be ready for a magnetic frame on the family refrigerator, but that's Invulnerability speaking, not the real you! So, let's show you off.

Someone with fresh eyes who can view your flower diagram objectively, can also provide you with insights you likely never considered. They may note depth and connections in your flower that completely eluded you. You can also think of it this way: Essentially, you are taking someone to the salad bar, showing them your offerings, and asking how they would combine them to create something unique and palatable. You're interested in creativity, not feasibility, at this point. You're looking for insights and novel combinations that get you thinking. You might not fancy ham and pineapple on pizza, but such an unusual combination sure gets you thinking!

When I displayed my flower diagram as part of a class exercise, a student saw possibilities in my flower diagram that I had never even considered. This student mixed and matched petals and suggested that I could work with a computer science professor to create a healthy eating video for children using canine characters. In doing so, I would connect my interest in learning more about technology with my wish to engage in collaborative work with my colleagues and create something that is suited to my discipline for a population I care deeply about, while also incorporating my love of dogs. What an awesome project to get me out of a work rut, point me down a new path, and help kids! Is that creative, or what?

This book started out as such a project, as well. How could I combine my love of writing, desire to help others, creativity, and talking about myself? I could write a book that helps others work past life challenges in an innovative way based on research and my own observations and experiences. Voila!

You and your consorts might come up with some pretty wacky ideas, as well. Maybe in combining your interests, you'll dream up a place where one can wash their horse while drinking beer and singing show tunes. You'd frequent that establishment if you had a horse, drank beer, and loved show tunes, wouldn't you? That sort of combination is evidence that the creative juices have really started flowing!

Think Picasso, not Rembrandt, at this point. Focus on creativity, not realism. The best way to come up with innovative ideas of how to construct a meaningful life path away from the hole is to develop a hundred ideas for various paths away from the hole. In fact, most research suggests that it's not until you eliminate *all* the average and ordinary ideas that the funky, fun, and fulfilling ones, the ones with true potential to propel you forward, emerge.

A fabulous way to get the creative juices flowing is to engage in play. Steven Johnson describes this phenomenon in his very enjoyable TED talk, "The playful wonderland behind great inventions."

It might tax your vulnerability fortitude, but show your flower diagram to at least three other people and ask them how they would mix-and-match the various segments to come up with new endeavors, activities, or jobs. This exercise is one-part continued vulnerability reinforcement and three-parts Process of learning (gaining additional insights), Active learning (asking questions and doing), and Curiosity (brainstorming new ideas) practice.

Write down the ideas you receive from others on the lines below, and then add at least ten (yes, *another ten*!) of your own ideas to the list. Remember, you are not shooting for practicality, financial potential, or even overall appeal at this point. If you'd like to incorporate additional interests that come to mind as you brainstorm, feel free, just be sure to add them as new petals to your flower, as well.

Based upon my flower diagram, I could:

_____
_____
_____
_____
_____
_____
_____
_____
_____
_____
_____
_____
_____
_____
_____
_____
_____
_____
_____
_____
_____
_____
_____
_____

Look back over your list. I'll bet there are some truly creative ideas there! You might not be ready to take out a second mortgage to open your show tune/horse-washing saloon, but whether you realize it or not, you've just significantly improved your eyesight. Had you ever envisioned any of those combinations before? No? Really? See, you have already expanded your horizons. You have opened your mind to new possibilities and vistas. Pursuing any of the ideas on your list would require you to take additional steps away from the hole.

~~~~~~~~~~~~~~~~~~~~

It's time to return to your new path progress checklist. Through the creation of your flower and consideration of novel combinations of petals, you have accomplished the third goal. You ROCK!! Go ahead and put a bright red check mark in the third box.

☰ gain comfort with the weak, imperfect, incompetent aspects of vulnerability
☰ expand your field of vision by trying something new
☐ develop and integrate your skill set
☐ align your skills with your values

~~~~~~~~~~~~~~~~~~~~

 **From here...**

The next goal involves crafting a unique path considerate of your integrated being. It's time to finish off that mocha, put the pillow back on the couch, stash your pen behind your ear, and put your walking shoes back on. You're getting down to business now.

CHAPTER 8 TRAIL MARKERS

An absence of interconnectedness among facets of your life yields a sense of overall disconnect and dissatisfaction.

The more of your true being you infuse into your existence, the more fulfilling your existence becomes.

The best way to come up with a novel idea of how to move beyond your stuck point is to construct numerous ideas.

CHAPTER 9

You be you

BY NOW, YOU'VE realized the ways society provided you with messages (shovels) that you internalized (dig holes) resulting in your feeling stuck and suffocated (the dirt you dig out becomes the walls that surround your hole and close you in). I've also told you about how your demons come to cohabit this space with you. Since you've made it this far, you've made substantial progress toward climbing out of your hole and defeating Invulnerability, Impostor Syndrome, and Risk and Failure Aversion. You've knocked down the dirt wall and focused your vision, enabling you to see clearly the wide-open horizon that lies in front of you. You've even begun contemplating what far-fetched yellow-brick-road paths might look like. You're on a roll!

In my estimation, you're ready to get even more serious. You've fortified your armor, significantly weakened or slayed your demons, and wrapped your mind around making your life as fulfilling as it can be. You've taken into consideration who you are as a multi-faceted and complex human. You've thought about what it would take to enrich your life in meaningful ways, and you've begun to recognize the utility of creating a more integrated and unified you.

See what I mean? Look at you go!

When you first began to address vulnerability, you took baby steps. You began with exposure to vulnerability to test the waters and grow your confidence levels. Eventually, you became more strategic in exercising your vulnerability. Then, through the creation of your flower, you reacquainted yourself with the various meaningful facets of your being. The flower petals and their various combinations and synergies will now serve as the paving stones for your new path. Essentially, you have identified and familiarized yourself with the process and tenets of creating a fulfilling life path.

Did you even realize how much you've accomplished? You're totally working the program!

Now, it's time to take it to a more strategic level.

You're probably thinking, "What should my life path be grounded upon?"

Look at you asking excellent questions! You really get it!

And, I'll tell you, too. Your new, fulfilling life path must be built upon your values. Real, true, honest, vulnerable, personal values. You know the molds cement is poured into to create steppingstone? Those molds are your values. They encapsulate and tie together the facets of your life around which you'll create your path. And only you can identify which you should retain and which have led you down the unfulfilling path.

First, of course, a cautionary story...

Indulge me a moment while I digress to share with you an anecdote about how your social conditioning may also affects your ability to stay true to your values and what is most meaningful to you.

Every semester I teach courses in Introduction to Psychology. Many professors hate teaching intro courses, but I love them. When executed effectively, it's like watching young kids exposed to magic for the first time.

Katherine Schulz and Jia Jiang provide excellent insights into the power inherent in recognizing risk and failure for what they really are – opportunities for growth.

Before our initial class session, I ask the students to watch "Music and Life" by Alan Watts along with four TED talks: Sir Ken Robinson's "Do Schools Kill Creativity," Brené Brown's "Listening to Shame," Kathryn Schulz's "On Being Wrong," and Jia Jiang's "What I Learned from 100 Days of Rejection."

There are so many fantastic talks I share throughout the semester, but these open the door to discussion about vulnerability, conditioning of classroom behaviors, values, risk-taking, and failure.

In an effort to make my Introduction to Psychology course more Human Nature 101, we start with an examination of their experiences in education. From my earlier rants, you know I am no fan of traditional conceptualizations of education. So, I strive to make my class different. Discussing the TED talks during our initial meeting helps establish that tone and hammers home that my course should not be seen as a "one-size-fits-all" experience.

Our first session is spent discussing the tone we'd all feel most comfortable setting in the classroom and establishing practices that will help them learn, based upon what they've gleaned from the videos. I continually emphasize genuine learning over content memorization. I also hammer home the need for student empowerment and recognition of their ability to assume agency and get their money's worth in a system that often expects relative passivity from them. Which is, you may have noticed, a position I've endorsed for you, too!

It may seem frivolous to some of my more content-focused colleagues, but in the Introduction to Psychology course, we spend the entire second half of our semester in small groups redesigning some facet of a new society.

The premise (which I took from the TV show, Last Man on Earth) is that the only survivors of a pandemic plague are the student and 999 others (including their group members), who have gathered together in Kansas City.

I purposefully begin the first meeting of small groups asking students to discuss a handout focusing on their life-guiding values. (There are several great online questionnaires that can help you do the same.)

To jump start your thinking about your values, take an online quiz. I like LifeValuesInventory.org. Another approach advocated by the authors of **Tribal Leadership***, involves recounting a challenge in your life then discerning the values that drove your actions.*

They then shift their focus to the values they hold for the facet of society on which they have elected to work - healthcare, education, family, etc.

Over the course of the next few weeks, groups research and debate the goals for their new society for the next one, five, and ten years. Among other exercises, I encourage them to speak with faculty members in different disciplines, their family members, and others to gain a deep appreciation of multiple perspectives on their topic. They develop a conceptual mind map for their area of focus (similar in many ways to the personal flower diagram you created) and integrate into it the feedback they receive.

All the time I reinforce that the plan they ultimately develop should be guided by their values.

Then, I say it again, for emphasis, "Guided by your values!"

After many hours of small group discussion and society development work, guess what happens when they present their plans at the end of the semester? Did you guess that they come up with astonishingly blissful, utopian communities? If so, you are waaaaay off-base.

Despite researching multiple historical, cultural, and even futuristic paradigms, and arguing over the merits and downsides of each from various perspectives, and often concocting something relatively unique for the first year, by the tenth year, their models are very similar to the present-day paradigms they confess to frequently complaining about.

I ask them, "What were your prevailing values?"

They respond with...

"Happiness..."

"Fulfillment..."

"Unity..."

"Efficiency..."

"Okay," I inquire. "How well does your new society facilitate the realization of such values?"

"Well, not so well..." is the typical response.

And, so, I ask, "Why?"

Their answers are revealing, and often perpetuate soul-searching in a way that hammers home everything I wanted them to glean from my method of instruction across the semester and carry with them through life.

Through a process of Socratic questioning, I ask them about the population's mental state. I ask them about how they, personally, would like to spend their first year with 999 strangers. I ask them what it would look like if their first year together was truly aligned with their values.

Eventually, someone asks the same of me, and I share with them that I would want to move the group to Malibu, eat avocados to my heart's content, and chill on the beach with no set agenda for the first year, while everyone got to know one another on relaxed terms and began to psychologically heal.

Their reactions are priceless.

"Well, of course, we'd rather relax on the beach for the first year and see how everyone gels."

"Of course, we'd all feel happier, more unified, and fulfilled, and the efficiency of our new society would develop in a more naturalistic and useful way if we spent the first year just getting to know one another." (That one may be a *bit* of a paraphrase.)

I ask them how their first year of college would have been different if they were given a month or so to just live with one another on campus with no pressure or agenda before orientation began. They usually love the idea.

"So, why," I ask, "did you not move the new tribe from Kansas City to Malibu, where the sun shines on the beach and the fruit and nut trees are plentiful and just lie low? Would you not have been happier? Would your society not have benefitted from such an approach?"

"But you didn't tell us that was an option."

At this point, the realization sets in that they haven't truly accepted the personal empowerment I attempted to bestow upon them. Nor have they conceptualized the challenge in light of their values. This leads to deeper recognition of the impact of their upbringing and the ways in which their vision has diminished over time. Despite all their research and debate, every one of them returns to the desire to give me what they thought I wanted to see from this assignment.

Yet I reiterate that what I wanted to see involved consideration of the concepts of psychology and human nature covered during the first half of the semester along with problem-solving exploration *guided by their personal values.*

I make clear, though, that their groups and every group that came before them, began at day one imposing a way of life on the new society that ultimately morphed into the old way of life.

"You all fail."

Not really, but they understand my sense of humor by now.

Then, someone invariably says, "I guess we didn't think beyond our conditioning. Despite everything you taught us this semester, we returned to the way we've always done things, even when they were not aligned with our values and we gripe about them every day."

Then another astute student chimes in with, "We gave you what we thought you wanted, rather than stepping back and really understanding you, and the assignment, and considering our values and what *we* wanted."

The coup d'état comes when another student suggests, "I guess, when we face challenges, rather than just jumping in and solving them, based on prior conditioning and habits, we should take a step back and look at the bigger picture from multiple perspectives, and consider how our values can really drive our generation of solutions."

Then, I pat myself on the back.

Most of us split our time between things we *have*-to do and things we *want*-to do. The greater the overlap, the more fulfilled and happier we feel. The greater the distinction, the less fulfilled and happy we feel. Therefore, the goal is to modify the have-to activities to make them more want-to activities, and to shift the balance to ensure we maintain a majority of want-to or overlapping activities. My class had lost sight of the want-to's associated with their values. They had been conditioned over time to focus almost exclusively on the have-to's. This history leads them repeatedly down unfulfilling paths.

So, let's turn now to an examination of your have-to's and want-to's. The next few exercises are aimed at assessing your current balance and creating a more beneficial equilibrium in tune with your values.

Recognizing the role of values

As you've no doubt figured out by now, you got your first nudge onto your life path by others in your life.

"What do you want to be when you grow up, Susie?" comes with the implicit suggestion that Susie figure things out, select a career from the acceptable list of options, chart a course, and stay that course. "An, astronaut, you say? Well, bless your heart." That's some pressure for a six-year-old! No wonder so many of us end up feeling stifled in middle management positions!

Well, maybe at forty-five-years-old and six-foot-three, you weren't destined to become an astronaut, after all. Does that mean you can't keep your head in the clouds in some way? Of course not! But society (and maybe your parents, significant other, and boss) don't get why you still have a longing to star gaze. Such activities might not propel you toward societally-defined success, but a complete absence of such enjoyable activities does promote unhappiness.

How closely have your values informed your life path? Most of us, or at least those of us who eventually end up feeling trapped in our lives or unsure of where to go next, experience a disconnect between our values and the activities along our life path. Hence, you might guess that I'm going to ask you next to consider your values.

To ensure you create a path aligned with what instills meaning in your life, a good place to begin involves distinguishing those activities that "drain" you, from those which "sustain" you.

There's a mighty good chance that once you develop your list, the reason you are feeling so stymied or suffocated will become increasingly clear. And it's not just because you'll note a multitude of draining activities or that you spend the majority of your time involved in draining activities; it's because the activities you've identified as draining are considered so because they are not in line with your values.

You'll move along one step at a time. This is going to be an organization-intensive chapter. Stretch your fingers and gather up your highlighters and glitter pen.

Begin by listing all the activities you spend most of your time doing, along with those you would like to spend time on.

A good place to begin is with your flower. Then, return to your "List of things to not forget that I like" and pencil those in. Finally, turn to your Past/Present/Future exercise, and then examine any additional notes you've made in the margins of this book or in your journal to round out your list.

Ultimately, the list should encompass, as closely as possible, the ways you spend your time and the ways you'd *like* to spend your time. Include your desire petal activities here, as well. You can use your glitter pen again or just put an asterisk beside those activities.

After you make your list, I'll discuss the D/S column and the values.

Activities List:

1. D/S___
   Activity:_____

   _____
   _____
   Values:_____
   _____

2. D/S___
   Activity:_____

   _____
   _____
   Values:_____
   _____

3. D/S___
   Activity:_____

   _____
   _____
   Values:_____
   _____

4. D/S___
   Activity:_____

   _____
   _____
   Values:_____
   _____

5. D/S___
   Activity:_____

   _____
   _____
   Values:_____
   _____
   _____

6. D/S____
   Activity:_____

   _____

   _____

   Values:_____

   _____

   _____

7. D/S____
   Activity:_____

   _____

   _____

   Values:_____

   _____

   _____

8. D/S____
   Activity:_____

   _____

   _____

   Values:_____

   _____

   _____

9. D/S____
   Activity:_____

   _____

   _____

   Values:_____

   _____

   _____

10. D/S____
   Activity:_____

   _____

   _____

   Values:_____

   _____

   _____

11. D/S___

Activity:_____

_____

_____

Values:_____

_____

_____

12. D/S___

Activity:_____

_____

_____

Values:_____

_____

_____

13. D/S___

Activity:_____

_____

_____

Values:_____

_____

_____

14. D/S___

Activity:_____

_____

_____

Values:_____

_____

_____

15. D/S___

Activity:_____

_____

_____

Values:_____

_____

_____

16. D/S____

    Activity:_____

    _____

    _____

    Values:_____

    _____

    _____

Feel free to add in an additional piece of paper, if needed, to capture all your activities.

Once you've completed your list, go through it and designate each activity as "D" (draining) or "S" (sustaining). If you reach an activity that is difficult to classify, or ambiguous because it involves elements of both D and S, see if you can break it down into components and mark each component accordingly.

The next step involves identifying the personally held values that promote your engagement in each activity.

To assist you in clarifying your guiding values, refer to Table 1. While this chart combines the majority of values identified in research, feel free to add any additional values you feel capture the true reason for your engagement in an activity.

As you go down your list, you may find that some of your actions are guided by more than one value. If so, list more than one.

However, if you find yourself identifying more than three values for any given activity, try to isolate the one or two that seem most relevant and stick with those.

As an additional visual, for those of you into such things as much as I am, you can color code the D and S values behind each activity on the Table. For instance, put a yellow highlight hashmark next to a value every time you designate it as associated with a draining activity. Put a different color hashmark (I like a pink highlighter because it signifies happiness to me) next to the values you associate with sustaining activities. Doing this can help you identify patterns when you've completed this task.

Oh... one more thing, when you identify values associated with any desire petals/activities, make sure you establish a special notation for them. Go ahead and use that glitter pen!

After you've matched your values with your draining and sustaining activities, step away for a little while. Then, come back later and reassess your list. Are you still in agreement with your three-hours ago or yesterday self? If so, fabulous! If not, think carefully and make any modifications you deem necessary.

Table 1: Commonly Identified Personal Values

Concern for Family/Tribe	Belonging
Concern for Environment	Social Justice
Creativity/Expression of Self	Intimacy
Passion	Humility/Modesty
Achievement/Mastery/Accomplishment	Loyalty/Reliability/Dependability
Aesthetics/Beauty	Simple Pleasures/Contentment
Spirituality/Religion	Health and Well-being
Privacy/Alone Time	Responsibility
Resilience/Persistence/Determination	Stability/Routine/Predictability/Security
Precision/Efficiency/Order	Change/Variety/Spontaneity
Fast-pace/Deadlines/Pressure	Flexibility/Latitude
Power/Respect/Recognition	Competition with Self/Others
Adventure/Adrenaline Rush	Financial Prosperity
Independence/Self-reliance	Innovation/Entrepreneurship
Knowledge Acquisition/Critical Thinking/Problem-solving	Leadership/Influencing/Motivating/Persuading Others

A deeper values exploration

Looking over the values you associate with your draining and sustaining activities might reveal some things you enjoy just because they are fun – like dancing and playing with puppies. Other things you enjoy might not seem so light-hearted – like working through complex crossword puzzles or rebuilding car engines. Although these activities won't find you with a broad smile on your face for the duration, they demonstrate a value placed on intellectual challenges and they feed your soul. This is good to know.

When you fully appreciate what you value and what provides you with a sense of satisfaction and fulfillment, you can seek additional opportunities that expand your behavioral repertoire and reaffirm your authentic nature.

The more you can learn about yourself through the detection of patterns in your draining and sustaining activities, the more personalized and fulfilling you can make your lifepath.

Focus on your draining activities

You engage in draining activities for a variety of reasons that may align with your fulfilling life path or obstruct its development. Your draining activities likely include some you might not enjoy in their own right, but which, nonetheless, correspond to one of your higher-order values. Some may be just be necessary evils. Other draining activities, you'll realize were driven by the demons.

When Jack reflected on his work-related draining activities, he realized that although the tasks he highlighted don't all provide him an immediate sense of fulfillment, he does many of them because it pleases him to be seen as reliable. Jack also thinks highly of the institution he works for and values doing what he can to ensure it thrives.

This is the same reason I attend faculty meetings. I want to be a team-player, because cooperation and collaboration provide me a sense of fulfillment. Oh sure, it might not seem that way, from the excessive complaining I engage in before, during, and after these meetings, but it's not simply a sense of contractual obligation that drives my attendance.

On the other hand, Marin realized she picks up the slack around her office, often completing her employee's tasks, out of fear that anything not completed optimally will reflect poorly on her. Essentially, she completes many of her draining activities due to demon-driven fears about her needs for safety and security. When Marin considers her limited sustaining activities, it becomes increasingly evident that such a mindset is at odds with creating her fulfilling life path.

The primary difference, and the point to discern involves whether you engage in an activity out of fear or to avoid an adverse consequence (Marin's demon-driven safety-related draining activity) or because you reap some measure of joy from engagement (Risa and Jack's draining activities that nevertheless made them feel like valued, reliable, and collaborative members of their academic communities).

I'm going to go out on a limb now and hypothesize that, like Marin, some of the values associated with your draining activities are also vestiges of the demon voices (internalized messages of what you *should* value and how you *should* behave). You might still hear some of these messages on a daily basis from your boss, your parents, or your significant other. It's important to take note of these and decide how to address them.

Of course, there are likely obligatory draining activities on your list that you engage in simply to put food on the table, avoid being thrown in jail for tax evasion, or prevent ants from taking over your kitchen. It's natural that you will not feel fulfilled, sustained, and satisfied by every activity you engage in. Some things will always be chores.

As much as possible, though, it will serve you well to determine whether you are engaging in a draining activity because it is consistent with a higher-order sustaining value, a necessary evil, or because there are still demon voices echoing in your head.

Drudgery draining activities:

For the necessary evil draining activities, an attitude adjustment may help reduce the level of the drudgery. Remind yourself that the ten-hours a week you spend chauffeuring your children to various lessons, helps them develop their talents and become well-rounded humans.

Potentially, tasks that can't be made less draining through reframing or attitude adjustments could be delegated.

Might the money you save doing your own taxes (a value of frugality – which, in this instance, drives a sense of drain) be compensated for by the time and peace of mind you gain through hiring a tax accountant (a value of contentment – which, in this case could result in feeling sustained)?

Perhaps the fear, trepidation, and premature sense of drain you feel in visiting the dentist (with which I completely identify) could be ameliorated to some degree by listening to music?

The main point is that there will be some pure and simple chores on your draining list you just can't or shouldn't eliminate. Apply your Curiosity and creativity, along with your Active problem-solving skills, to reduce the drudgery wherever possible.

Demon-driven draining Activities:

The other concerning draining activities are driven by the demon voices of internalized messages.

It's critically important to recognize these for what they are. Entire books in the realm of cognitive therapy have been written on how to defeat self-sabotaging thoughts.

By now, though, you have engaged in substantial work to recognize and counter Impostor Syndrome, Invulnerability, and Risk and Failure Aversion. I feel confident that you can identify those values driven by external forces rather than those consistent with how you see your true, genuine, and authentic self.

~~~~~~~~~~~~~~~~~~~~

Caveat: Bear in mind that values should not be judgment-laden. There is no one-size-fits-all values collection, despite what society might tell you. There's nothing wrong with being guided by a value of Financial Prosperity or Competition with Others, for instance, so long as these values sustain you.

It's only when you are guided by values poorly aligned with your internal motivators and moral compass that you feel a sense of drain.

There have been times in my past when I valued Belonging over Privacy and Alone Time because I felt a pull from my environment to be social and extroverted. I grew to believe my true introvert tendencies were a handicap and forced myself to try and fit in. I went to great pains (literally, it seemed) to attend group functions, to mingle at parties, to browse outdoor art festivals. Every time I left feeling drained.

On the other hand, my mother and daughter, natural extroverts, feel sustained and reap great enjoyment from these same sorts of activities.

~~~~~~~~~~~~~~~~~~~~

Focus on your sustaining activities

While you may not be able to engage solely in sustaining activities, it is useful to recognize themes associated with what sustains you. Unless you are already a billionaire, you're probably not going to ever completely escape the dirty work. If it makes you feel any better, I'll bet the billionaires probably still need to deal with lawsuits. And, really, who needs that?

Is it fair to say, though, that the activities on your sustaining list are ones you'd continue doing even if you won a billion-dollar lottery tomorrow? If there is anything on the sustaining activities list that you would NOT continue doing if you won a billion-dollar lottery, strike through or erase it. You're not looking for the *"meh"* activities. You're looking for those that truly provide you a sense of satisfaction, joy, and fulfillment.

What does the resulting list say about you?

The combination of values associated with your sustaining activities will serve as beacons on your new path. Just like you might set your sights on Denver, and there may be two exits and a right turn involved in getting you from your starting point A to that ending point B, your values will serve as road signs guiding you from one sustaining stop to the next along your fulfilling path.

Now for the insight

Which values did you list, in order of frequency of appearance, for your **sustaining** activities?

1. _____
2. _____
3. _____
4. _____
5. _____
6. _____
7. _____
8. _____

If you included **Desire** activities, which values did you list, in order of frequency of appearance, for them?

1. _____
2. _____
3. _____
4. _____
5. _____
6. _____
7. _____
8. _____

When you take a bird's eye view of these lists, what do you see? What themes do you notice? Is there a clear preference for privacy and alone time? Do you gain fulfillment most from those activities that involve adventure? Are you an extroverted person who thrives in upholding social justice? Do you desire to infuse creativity and self-expression into your life? Which, if any, values are important to you, but only show up through your desire activities?

To formulate a life path true to your authentic self, you need to emphasize activities driven by heart-felt values. They will serve as pushpins on your life path map. The steps along your new path, some of which might be scary or tedious, are made bearable when you recognize their inherent contribution to who you truly are and wish to be.

Sustaining and desire values serve as GPS coordinates on the fulfilling life path. These are the beacons you want to be most pronounced. For this reason, you'll want to begin brainstorming additional activities aligned with each value. These will constitute the scenic vistas awaiting you at each stop. They're what you'll have to look forward to with each step you take.

~~~~~~~~~~~~~~~~~~~~

Return to your progress checklist. You're checking off the LAST box! Pause for a moment and do a little end-zone happy dance. That's it! You go, friend!

Now, all that remains is charting your path. In the next chapters we'll address putting in the pushpins. In the meantime, get your glitter pen back out and mark off that fourth box!!

- ▤ gain comfort with the weak, imperfect, incompetent aspects of vulnerability
- ▤ expand your field of vision by trying something new
- ▤ develop and integrate your skill set
- ☐ align your skills with your values

~~~~~~~~~~~~~~~~~~~~

From here...

Whew - that was a LOT of work! But, you're well on your way to constructing a more fulfilling life path. Now you can turn your attention to the scope of your path. Are you going to visit all of Italy in a week? Or are you going to focus on Rome? Or, maybe you feel compelled to spend a month in Rome, then a week in Venice and Sicily.

Which approach is best tailored to you?

Keep reading and give it some thought. One thing is certain though, you cannot and will not travel down this path as part of an itinerary-driven, organized group of same-color t-shirt-wearing folks following the guy with a yellow flag on a stick.

This new path is all YOU, baby!

CHAPTER 9 TRAIL MARKERS

Which values guide your engagement in draining versus sustaining life activities?

The three forms of draining activities include 1) those aligned with higher-order sustaining values, 2) those which are necessary evils, and 3) those which are remnants of the demon voices.

Values that sustain you should serve as your GPS points in the creation of your fulfilling life path.

Your own yellow brick road

THIS IS THE LAST step. Can you believe it? Can you believe how far you've come? I hope you are thrilled with and proud of your progress. I'm sure proud of you! Now it's time to put all your thoughtful learning into play.

In this chapter, I'll provide an overview of path trajectories for you to consider.

As a quick review, I've discussed the necessity of integrating various facets of your being, whenever possible. You've explored what you do and why you do it. You've covered the need to strike a beneficial balance between those activities that drain and those that sustain.

You've also learned that it serves you well to emphasize the aspects of draining tasks that align with your heart-felt values, while eliminating or modifying to the extent possible, those that are demon-driven. Since you are comfortable now with vulnerability and experimentation, it's time to try new things and explore new terrain. You're ready to formulate a path based on your insights and GPS coordinates.

This is the point at which, if you were visiting me for weekly therapy, we might move to every other week. The heaviest lifting is behind you now. You and I are on the same page. Around this time, I would also encourage you to become more independent and break away from my support.

~~~~~~~~~~~~~~~~~~~~

A CAUTION for my fellow researchers, planners, list-makers, and
all-round Type A personality brethren:

When I planned my honeymoon back in the early 1990's, I bought
every travel guide for Barbados known to man. Before planning a single detail, I had read, highlighted, and made notes in the margins of
each one of them. I could tell you how to get from any point on the
island to any other point along with the literacy rate of Barbados. I
knew which activities we would do on which days and the best times
of day to do each. Some might say I'm a bit obsessive in my planning.
To that I say, "Whatever."

I'm willing to stake my current TripAdvisor reputation on the likelihood that some readers of this book may appreciate a detailed itin-
erary as much as I do. So, I want to make sure you hear me loud and
clear when I tell you this fulfilling life path you're about to create
should NOT be overly detailed or chiseled in stone! There absolutely,
positively MUST be room for you to remain agile.

While you might set a course for a destination you can reach in
two years or five years, let's make sure you remain focused on the
process, NOT the destination. Continue to self-monitor to make sure
you don't pick up a shovel along the way.

If you forget, look back at that tattoo you got a few weeks ago,
"*Learning is a process, not a destination.*"

~~~~~~~~~~~~~~~~~~~~

You are about to enter a more exploratory life path construction
phase.

With an understanding of how your life hole was dug, an appreciation of the messages that served as your shovels, and identification
of the demon(s) that caused you the greatest difficulty, you have been
able to step back and objectively examine your life and actions.

Equipped as you are now with essential self-knowledge, I feel totally confident you can move into path construction with limited guidance.

Various types of paths

I've known people everywhere I've lived who have never left their state, their region, or their country. I suspect it's because most of them find what sustains and fulfills them close to home. Nevertheless, if they decided to take a trip, I probably would not start them off with a trek up the Himalayas. The same holds true for you. I know you're excited to get moving, but let's proceed thoughtfully.

You'll want to tailor your path to your own unique values, goals, and constellation of sustaining and desire activities. Marin, Jack, and I each had somewhat different challenges that required conscious deliberation as we constructed our paths.

Below, I've outlined four different path trajectories. They are all variations on the theme. You may find you identify closely with one of them or you may wish to integrate various aspects of the different approaches.

The four paths include:

1. The Radical Departure Approach: This approach is best suited to people entrenched in an existential life crisis. This person knows what they DON'T want any more, but aren't sure what they DO want. They need help creating a new life path that gets them out of the trench they've been living in.

2. The Radical Exploratory Approach: This approach is best for people who have great room for personal growth. This individual may just be starting out in life or may have lived a longer, more sheltered life. They have goals for personal development but are unclear as to how to create an exploratory, growth-centered life path.

3. The Single-Facet Departure Approach: This approach is best suited for people who are generally content with their lives in all ways but one. While their love life is great, their professional life is a disappointment. Or, vice versa. After a while, having one primary facet of life out of balance with the other facets makes that problematic area seems all the more pronounced and troublesome.

4. The Conscious Exploration Approach: This approach is best for people who lose sight of the path altogether. These folks often have a ladder with checklists at each rung, rather than a scenic life path. They've grown tired of the climb and are looking for ways to enjoy life before it's too late.

Each course requires a slightly different strategy. As I present each in turn, I'll discuss the facets of the PACT and how they influence path development. Keep your journal handy or put some sticky tabs on the pages listing your values, and your sustaining and desire activities. You'll refer back to them throughout the next few chapters.

I'd suggest you skim through each of the four approaches before carefully considering which one(s) presents the closest fit to your situation. Then, go back and really study the path construction advice presented in the relevant chapter(s).

> *After you decide on a path approach,*
> *wait a few days before acting on it.*
> *When you revisit the plan, are you*
> *still excited about it? Are you nervous*
> *or anxious?*

When you decide on an approach, follow the guidelines and create your own personalized plan. Then, wait a few days before acting on it and revisit the plan. Are you still excited about it? Are you nervous or anxious?

If you feel you need to make any modifications before you begin, do so at this point. But, think carefully about why you've decided to make those changes. Are you confident you're making them to craft a plan better aligned to your goals and values? Or, are you back-peddling because you think you hear the demons chanting taunts?

Gain clarity on this issue, and then steel your resolve to move forward.

 From here...

Wow! I sort of feel like I'm releasing a butterfly. When I think of all you've accomplished since page one, I can imagine no better analogy than that of a caterpillar transforming into a beautiful butterfly.

Where will you go as you take flight? How awesome is it to know the world is open for your exploration?

The next few chapters will propose variations of path construction for you to consider. Decide which one(s) best suit your growth trajectory, then spread your wings, and FLY!

CHAPTER 10 TRAIL MARKERS

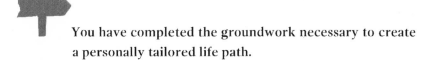

You have completed the groundwork necessary to create a personally tailored life path.

Only you can decide where to go from here. Which path best suits your goals, desires, and values?

CHAPTER 11

The Radical Departure approach

YOU'VE NO DOUBT heard stories about people who felt their lives were overwhelmingly draining and who decided they needed a do-over. If this is the hole you currently find yourself in, you've probably also experienced a few unsustainable glimpses of joy along the way. Their contrast with your day-to-day doldrums, however, likely brought you to the realization that your current path is way off-track. If you're in need of a Radical Departure, you've reached the breaking point and may feel the need to scrap it all and make a fresh start.

If you're one of the folks in need of a general life overhaul, you won't be fulfilled by minor life tweaks. Remember way back in an early chapter, when I said your frustration might not have reached volcanic proportions? Well, if you *have* reached volcanic proportions, this approach is for you. Prior to your journey through this book, you likely fluctuated between feelings of depression, hopelessness, and being lost. By now, however, you have increased your understanding of how you reached that point. You've also learned quite a bit about yourself and how you remained stuck in such a suffocating hole.

To create your radically new life path, you're going to have to emphasize Thoughtfulness.

In other words, rather than buying a sports car and a gold chain in a quest for fulfilling change, it will serve you better to spend your time and energy considering how to tailor a path specific to your desires, goals, and values. The last thing someone searching for a radical new path needs is a fruitless trek. As examples of the Radical Departure approach, think about Cheryl Strayed's journey in *Wild* and Elizabeth Gilbert's exploration in *Eat, Pray, Love*. If you, however, are unable to drop everything and travel the world, you will need to determine another exploratory route.

Your first step is to return to the value analysis. I'm willing to bet your balance sheet is heavily weighted toward draining activities. Moreover, the majority of those draining activities are probably guided by societally-imposed, demon-driven values rather than authentic drudgery ones.

Charting your path

To ensure you've exorcised the demon(s) haunting your thoughts and actions, you'll want to take a direct tact. Without the demon-monkeys on your back, you'll be freed-up to create a more personalized path toward self-discovery.

Begin by formally breaking up with your most troubling demon. You can write it out as a "It's not you, it's me" kiss-off speech. Or maybe just a "hands over your ears and eyes shut" mantra. Perhaps all you need is a sign that reads, "I'm done with you, Failure Aversion! Good riddance!" You could make it your screen saver, write it in bright red lipstick on your bathroom mirror, or get another tattoo. Either way, write out your Dear John-esque note to the demon, or your new mantra, and refer back to it when you need a boost.

_____

_____

_____

_____

_____

_____

_____

_____

Stein

The next step in developing a Radical Departure life path involves clearing the weeds so you can focus on those activities best aligned with what you know to be the authentic you. The challenge is ensuring you pull the weeds out by the roots, while retaining the fruit-bearing plants and fragrant flowers.

Once the path is weeded and you have eliminated as many remnants of demon-guided activities as possible, you're probably going to be left with well-churned topsoil, lots of gaping holes, and quite a bit of leftover fertilizer. Don't despair! See this for what it truly is... a path ripe for cultivation. Where you may have previously tried to plant seeds in weed-infested, nutrient-deprived, dry earth, you now have before you an open landscape welcoming to new seed!

The Process focus in the Radical Departure approach rests on enjoying the fact-finding mission and living the values most fortifying to you. Cheryl Strayed and Elizabeth Gilbert didn't craft life-changing journeys around heavily detailed, itinerary-driven trips. They realized that the most rewarding aspect of the Radical Departure is the journey itself. However, they also recognized they could maximize the reward they reaped from their journeys by programming in certain GPS coordinates before taking their first steps.

Both women set GPS coordinates based on hypothesized alignment with their values and what they thought would grow. Their treks to each point served as experiments, and their arrival at each coordinate prompted reflection that either validated or nullified their assumptions. Either way, they ended up learning a great deal about themselves.

The key to a successful Radical Departure involves formulating a sense of purpose for the journey (aligning your life path with your values); beginning with a few GPS points that test your assumptions;

and, reflecting after each stop to recalibrate, nourish new plant growth, pull any emerging weeds, and set new coordinates.

While you have learned a great deal over the past few months, your future path remains open to discovery. The process of learning and path progression can't be completely preprogrammed, it must be approached with an openness to experience. There's a reason Cheryl Strayed and Elizabeth Gilbert chose the launching points they chose, but left many details of their trips open. They designed their points of departure to correspond with values they wanted to infuse into their lives, and then trusted that Active participation, guided by Thoughtful Curiosity, would elucidate the most fulfilling journey.

There may be aspects of your life that regardless of fit, must factor into the creation of your new journey. A job offer in New Zealand could really tempt the genuine you, but if one of your few sustaining activities is spending time with your children, whom your ex has primary custody of, you don't want to lose that. So, the Radical Departure approach begins with a search for any plants (or babies in the bath water) you don't want to dispense with. Consider any GPS points that must be pre-programmed into your life path and write them out here.

Path Confines:

_____

_____

_____

_____

_____

_____

So... where will you begin? This is a good point to stop and consider which aspects of your life path you want to prioritize. Once you identify the top three areas to explore and develop, consider the values that previously guided them. It is important to replace each of these with one of the sustaining or desire related values you previously identified to ensure your new path doesn't start veering off in unful-filling directions.

My top areas of personal development/goals:

1. _____

    Previous guiding values: _____

    _____

    _____

    New guiding values: _____

    _____

    _____

2. _____

    Previous guiding values: _____

    _____

    _____

    New guiding values: _____

    _____

    _____

3. _____

    Previous guiding values: _____

    _____

    _____

    New guiding values: _____

    _____

    _____

If you try to find a new job, a new relationship, a new social group, and on and on, all at once, you're going to become overwhelmed very quickly. So, turn your attention to prioritizing your goals for your new life path. Is there any sense of demon-driven obligation leaking into this thought process? You probably can't completely toss all your obligations, but when you review your goals, do #2 or #3 excite you more than goal #1? If so, I suggest you start with one of them. You can work in the obligatory goals once you've planted a few flowers and your path becomes increasingly appealing.

When you've decided upon a starting goal, list out five potential GPS points from your sustaining and desire activities list, or create new activities that align with this goal and its associated values. Since they are tentative, be sure to write them in pencil.

Goal: _____

Initial tentative GPS coordinates:

1. _____
   Reflection: _____
   _____
   _____
   _____

2. _____
   Reflection: _____
   _____
   _____
   _____

3. _____
   Reflection: _____
   _____
   _____
   _____

4. _____

    Reflection: _____

    _____

    _____

    _____

5. _____

    Reflection: _____

    _____

    _____

    _____

Choose one to start your journey then reflect and note whether any recalibration of the remaining activities is necessary. You might find that your original assumptions were wrong. If so, you will want to reconsider your next tentatively programmed stops. Upon engaging in an activity, and recalibrating your remaining experiences, add an additional GPS point.

Upon completion of the second experiment, reflect once more and modify the remaining original and newly added points, as needed. Continue adding activities to ensure you retain a running list of five experiential destinations. You'll need to continue this iterative exercise in your journal or on an erasable board. Take copious notes about what you find sustaining both in terms of the activity itself and the value underpinning it. To the extent possible, try to retain these activities and make them a daily part of your routine.

Address the other goals in the same fashion once the flora begins to bloom along the path of your first goal.

This is the Active part of the life path development Process. Essentially, you are testing growth hypotheses to determine whether seeds will blossom into beautiful plants or into stinkweeds, before becoming overly invested in them.

Here's how this process might look if you are searching for a new fulfilling career. You examine your values and realize that you'd like a career that involves being around other people, working to preserve the environment, and high adventure activities. So, you make your first GPS point into a fact gathering mission involving sharing these values with others and reflecting on their suggestions. Someone suggests that maybe a job with Greenpeace is your calling. Does Greenpeace sound appealing to you? Great. Your second GPS coordinate will involve ordering Greenpeace material. Then, you'll make a new contact and take a Greenpeace employee out to coffee to test your assumptions about their job and the work environment.

While you sip your latte, you'll realize that it's in your best interest to keep an open-mind and you'll decide to ask this like-minded person about other jobs they considered and what they find valuable about the work they do at Greenpeace. Could there be additional GPS coordinates you want to explore before trekking further down the Greenpeace path?

Did your new Greenpeace friend invite you to an information session or a rally? Cool! Go! Maybe you'll find it's a perfect fit. Maybe, like sushi, you'll find it's really not for you. Either way, reflect on what you liked and what made it a less than optimal fit. Then, add the positive qualities to your flower, and investigate the other possibilities that have recently emerged through your process of exploration.

After some time of meeting people, making new connections, demonstrating your receptivity, and trying out new activities, maximally sustaining opportunities will be revealed. Until then, treat each as a potential new GPS point and experiment.

You may need to refer back to your mantra or Dear John letter from time to time. There's no shame in that. Demons, like weeds, are tough to eradicate in an organically grown garden.

~~~~~~~~~~~~~~~~~~~~

Another CAUTION...

Do not treat the first new exciting opportunity as THE golden road. I know you've been frustrated for far too long but take your time and shop around. Ensuring you find a job, a significant other, and/or a leisure time pursuit that most closely aligns with your sustaining values requires an open mind. By the way, you needn't compartmentalize these areas. Remember, each recalibration should also be a consideration of how your subsequent experiences can integrate the meaningful facets of your being, which you may have just discovered.

~~~~~~~~~~~~~~~~~~~~~~

After you've completed several activities associated with your first goal, consider means of integrating activities aligned with your second goal. Ask yourself which, if any, activities from your list would address both goals #1 and #2? Incorporate those activities into your repertoire. The last thing you want to do is develop three completely distinct trajectories. Remember, you are not a salad bar. Remain committed to infusing your genuine self, and all the related values and sustaining activities into all facets of your life.

With additional experiences under your belt and an increased understanding of what moves you along your fulfilling path, begin integrating activities associated with goal #3.

Concrete steps:

1. Identify your externally imposed life constraints.

2. Create arguments to counter the most overwhelming messages from your most annoying demon. Write those arguments out for future reference.

3. Identify your goals and prioritize them. It may seem less overwhelming to break path construction into manageable chunks.

4. Delineate the values that guided you in the past and the new ones that will serve as the foundation for your newly established goals.

5. Match your list of current sustaining and desire activities to the values guiding each goal then add additional potentially sustaining and desire activities.

6. Begin experimenting with various goal activities. Reflect and modify subsequent activities as needed. Repeat with your remaining goals.

7. Modify your GPS coordinates as needed. Hone your path and eliminate the activities that didn't bear the anticipated fruit.

CHAPTER 12

The Radical Exploration approach

WHEN YOUR ANGST is diffuse and your flower sparse, you'll want to start developing your path by engaging in a broad exploration. Recognizing all the avenues open to you can feel like Charlie stepping into Willy Wonka's chocolate world – overwhelming! Where do I even begin? There is so much to look at and so much to taste!

This is exactly how Marin felt. Although, like Charlie, she certainly felt a great measure of trepidation, she also found the experience very exhilarating. If you have led a sheltered life or one primarily dictated by the directives of other people, you may feel a bit giddy and anxious at this point. That's perfectly understandable. Fortunately, you now have the tools to move forward in creating your own personally-tailored, fulfilling life path.

You just need a plan of attack, so you don't wander aimlessly around the chocolate factory and end up in Oompa Loompa land.

Let's look more specifically at Marin's construction of her Radical Exploration path.

Marin reviewed her draining and sustaining activities and noted an overwhelming number of draining activities. Since she had gone directly from high school and motherhood to full-time employment, Marin spent years preoccupied with work performance and taking care of her daughter. She realized that she had never stopped to truly contemplate what she enjoyed or valued, beyond safety and security, so she honestly had very little insight into the personal values that would drive her sustaining activities.

Marin was so invested in her goal of achieving independence from her parents, that she couldn't see anything beyond that very narrow track. Her singular focus on safety and stability meant she neglected personal fulfillment and growth. Overall, she had restricted her life to a couple salad bar bins, providing little more than basic sustenance. Marin, unfortunately, had no discernable trajectory for her life. Her goals were obtuse and even contemplating where to begin intimidated and overwhelmed her.

Her review lead Marin to conclude that she wanted a fuller, more diversified life. Marin also recognized that the few sustaining activities she listed reflected her desire for adventure. However, adventure required she build her confidence. Above all else, Marin realized that she valued becoming a positive role model for her daughter.

While Marin's flower was sparse, she became resolute in her ambition to broaden her horizons. Her desire petals took on new meaning as sustaining activities, designed to boost her self-esteem and make her into the well-rounded person she sought to become. They also became the pushpins in the first arcs of Marin's path.

By creating a list of activities aligned with her values of "adventure" and "personal growth," and her goals of gaining confidence and becoming a positive role model for Christine, Marin was able to develop a hierarchy of activities to provide mastery experiences that would allow her to develop the progressive arcs that drove her to become increasingly daring.

Radical Departure vs. Radical Exploration

You may still wonder whether the Radical Departure approach or the Radical Exploration approach is right for you.

The Radical Departure is geared toward people with a wealth of life experiences that help them appreciate the ways in which their current path does *not* provide fulfillment. The Radical Exploration approach is designed for individuals with a dearth of life experiences. Like Marin, people in need of a Radical Exploration approach know they want more out of life, but their lack of experiences leaves them at a loss as to how to conceptualize crafting a new life path. The Radical Explorer hasn't sufficient life experiences to provide direction whereas Cheryl Strayed and Elizabeth Gilbert, in following a Radical Departure approach, at least appreciated where they were not interested in going.

Marin's path

Marin recognized that her time spent engaged in draining activities far outweighed her involvement in sustaining activities. To avoid becoming overwhelmed, and to ensure she was able to adequately reflect upon and learn from her novel experiences, Marin began by taking baby-steps. Ultimately, her life path looked like a reverberating radar signal.

She started small as she worked to build her self-confidence, engage in extensive self-discovery, and assemble a catalog of sustaining activities. The first arcs she drew involved exploring areas Invulnerability and Failure Aversion had prevented her from appreciating. By tackling her self-perceived weakest spots first, Marin was able to clarify her vision for the next waves. Still, as she moved from arc to arc, Marin wasn't sure what the third or fourth waves out would hold in store. She simply trusted the process, reflected extensively, and enjoyed the stroll.

In reviewing her accomplishments, Marin recognized the myriad steps she'd already taken to defeat Invulnerability and become increasingly Risk and Failure tolerant. This review alone gave her the confidence she needed to tackle the first wave.

Marin stoked her new-found self-assurance by joining Toast Masters and improving her public speaking skills. Since she envisioned herself becoming a more interesting, multifaceted individual, she made visiting area museums and attending free-talks at her local library into additional first-wave pushpins. These activities provided growth experiences, while still allowing her to feel safe.

Once she felt comfortable in these settings and her confidence bloomed, Marin pursued the second arc.

Here, Marin invested time in free online courses offered through Ivy League universities. She approached each new exploration with vulnerability and curiosity. She divulged her personal growth process to others, asked questions of the new people she met, and graciously accepted introductions along with invitations to activities. Marin rarely turned down opportunities for new experiences.

Several months later, and by the third wave, Marin had grown as a person and felt far more satisfied with her life. Still, she continued running experiments, developing her skill set, and meeting new people.

Marin's path centered on a process of on-going exploration and recalibration. She kept her day job, but along the way enjoyed numerous introductions and made a variety of connections. These folks took note of Marin's willingness to learn and grow, and she developed a broad range of social and professional connections, all of whom made her journey much more satisfying.

Marin's eventual fulfillment was a direct result of constructing an ever-widening path aligned with the PACT. Marin engaged in the

Stein

Process of learning by becoming an Active participant driven by Curiosity in a Thoughtful manner. Ultimately, Marin created an enjoyable exploratory life path. She erects few walls and has remained open to pursuing opportunities that address her most important life value - becoming an interesting and authentically self-assured person, one Christine can look up to.

Charting your path

When you are ready to explore, develop your first two arcs by considering the predominant values associated with your previously identified sustaining and desire activities. Next consider your primary goals. Alternatively, you may find it easier to write out your goals first, and the values second. Then, you can move into selecting or brainstorming activities that merge the two. Utilize as many lines as necessary to fully flesh out activities associated with each goal and value.

Value ➡ Activity ➡ Goal

(Personal growth)   (Visiting museums)   (Becoming interesting)

Now, highlight the activities from this list that seem most attractive. Rate the highlighted activities based on how daunting they seem. The least daunting should be approached in your first wave. The more challenging or intimidating activities can be saved for later waves. They may end up being modified before you even get to them.

Create a plan for the first two waves but no further out than that. Each wave should consist of at least two or three activities corresponding to your personal goals and matched with your values. You needn't try to address every personal goal or value in the first two waves. Of course, some activities might also help propel you toward more than one personal goal at a time.

With each wave's activities completed, reflect on your experiences. What did you learn? How have you grown? What have you found sustaining? What was not nearly as enjoyable or fulfilling as you expected it to be? Why was that the case?

Upon reflection, amend your list of activities associated with your goals and values, if need be. Create the next wave of activities as you see fit based upon your recalibrated list and repeat the process. Plan. Execute. Reflect. Repeat.

Each wave you complete should leave you feeling stronger and more empowered. For this reason, you'll need to step up the challenge a bit each round. Consider this when designing the activities and experiments for subsequent waves.

If you were unable to keep the demon voices at bay while engaging in a certain activity, then back-off that one and reflect on ways to make it more approachable. Perhaps your self-confidence sky-rocketed after a few great experiences and in your exuberant state you pushed ahead too quickly. Don't let an unanticipated difficulty set you back or diminish your progress.

There are no mistakes, only
learning opportunities.

Just as you did with building and strengthening your vulnerability muscle, you will do the same in fortifying yourself against Risk and Failure Aversion. Sometimes we think we can climb over a boulder, only to find we must chip away at it first, before it becomes surmountable. There is absolutely NO shame in taking your time. Remember, this is, first and foremost, a Process.

As you refine your approach, you might find your arcs branch off to address various facets of your personal development. Feel free to follow the protocol to explore employment, romantic relationships, social life, etc. With each wave, you should become a bit more daring and experimental. You'll find that mastery builds confidence, which opens news doors and reveals additional unforeseen growth opportunities.

Concrete steps:

1. Recognize that the Radical Exploration path is geared toward making the overwhelming wide-open horizon more manageable.

2. Consider, then write down, your values and personal goals.

3. Contemplate which of your sustaining and desire activities will bridge the gap between your values and your goals. If your current list of activities falls short of creating a conduit, brainstorm additional activities that will.

4. Once completed, rate each activity based on how daunting it seems. The least daunting should be approached in your first wave. The more challenging or intimidating activities can be saved for subsequent waves.

5. Create a tentative plan for the first two waves, but no farther out than that.

6. With each completed activity, reflect on the experience and omit, modify, or add additional activities as needed.

7. Using your self-reflection, create the next wave of activities as you see fit, then repeat the process. Plan. Execute. Reflect. Repeat.

8. Each wave you complete should leave you feeling stronger and more empowered. So, step up the challenge a bit each round.

9. After completing several waves, it will likely be time to consider crafting a more focused path, aligned with what you've learned about yourself.

CHAPTER 13

The Single-Facet
Departure approach

SOMETIMES, IT SEEMS like life is grand. Other times, life is grand and you're doing amazing things, *except* for your job/love relationship/social relationships... When this sort of imbalance occurs, it can feel like a paper cut on your thumb – a pain that aggravates you every time you move your hand.

Or maybe your job/love relationship/social relationships have gone from annoying papercut to gangrenous appendage.

When one facet of life is out of balance, it can throw other areas off, as well. This is the position Jack found himself in.

He loved his family and friends and wouldn't change his relationships with them for the world. But his job was bringing him down, and that was impacting his self-image, which then bled over into his marital relationship and weighed down what should have been carefree, fun times with his family and friends.

Jack needed to exact some meaningful change in his work life.

Jack's plan

When Jack completed his draining and sustaining activities and values chart, it became clear he values being around people, providing a sense of direction for others, and the feeling of community his neighborhood and work provided. He also recognized that he enjoys physical pursuits, including time spent watching and participating in sports, alone time spent reading books about historical events, and simple recreational pleasures, like going to concerts.

While Jack's flower was rich and complex, he noted that his greatest work-related fulfillment was derived from activities involving mentoring and coaching kid's athletic teams. While none of this was earth-shattering news for Jack, it did reaffirm his values. It also revealed that the activities he spent a disproportionate amount of his time in, failed to incorporate those values.

Unfortunately for Jack, despite working at a school, most of his time and effort revolved around administrative duties. Moreover, consistent with the forces that drove him to dig his hole, Jack's sights were still set on earning an MBA, so as to move into higher administrative echelons.

Upon analyzing the values that were driving his engagement in draining activities, Jack identified the voices that propelled him along his early path. They had admonished him to "live up to your potential," "reach for the stars" and "don't let us down."

When he contemplated the disconnect between his personal values and the way he spent his time, Jack recognized the source of his angst. His hole was dug and his dirt wall fortified with concerns about underachievement. This insight prompted Jack to examine the ways the demons ensured that he lacked confidence to pursue a more authentic life. Through discussions with his wife and friends, Jack achieved the peace of mind he needed to banish the demon voices. These good people reassured him that they would love and cherish him no less if he never earned an MBA.

Once he put all the pieces together, Jack determined the best way to achieve personal fulfillment involved becoming a middle school teacher and coaching an athletic team. Of all the ways Jack could combine his sustaining activities to address his predominant values, this path excited him most.

Ultimately, he created a life where a significant amount of time he spent at work involved activities that brought him personal fulfillment, affording him a sense of accomplishment aligned with his values.

The Single-Facet Departure requires close and Thoughtful examination of the ways the draining life facet differs from the more satisfying facets.

While Jack was generally sustained in his love and social relationships, he was drained by his work. Once he reviewed the values that guided the sustaining aspects of his personal and work relationships, and compared them to the draining aspects associated with his job, the misalignment of his career with his values became clear.

Another way of looking at this problem is to ask yourself: "If the same values that sustain me in other facets of my life were applied to the problematic domain, what would it look like?"

When Jack thought creatively about how his job would be different when overlaid with his sustaining values, he was able to find alternatives within his current career. Essentially, Jack used his values as his GPS destination coordinates, and his current job as his starting point. He morphed his current career in the direction of his GPS values, and when he arrived at his destination, he was a teacher and coach.

Charting your path

Consider the facet of life that most troubles you. Whether it is your work, your romantic relationship, your social life, or something else, write out the draining activities associated with it.

Then, return to the exercises you completed in the You be You chapter and assess which values accompany these draining activities.

Follow up by examining the activities and values associated with those facets of your life that bring you pleasure and create a sense of fulfillment.

Unfulfilling aspect of my life: _____

Draining Activities	Associated Values
_____	_____
_____	_____
_____	_____
_____	_____

Most fulfilling aspect of my life: _____

Sustaining Activities	Associated Values
_____	_____
_____	_____
_____	_____
_____	_____

Now, consider how the activities for your unfulfilling life facet would change if guided by the same values associated with your most fulfilling facet.

What would these unfulfilling work/family/relationship activities look like, if the guiding values changed?

For Jack, it was clear. His work life would revolve more around interactions with students, which makes him feel good about giving back and having an impact on young lives.

Start with the values, then brainstorm activities to address them.

Make the unfulfilling facet fulfilling:

<u>Sustaining Values</u>   <u>Possible Activities</u>

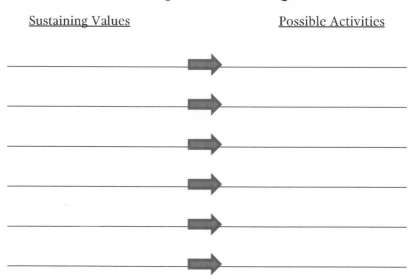

Occupational facet

While your process might not be as clear-cut as Jack's, returning to your Curiosity training can help you construct new activities associated with your sustaining values, making the unfulfilling part of your life more fulfilling.

Another way of approaching this task, if you are looking for a more drastic change, is to ask yourself: "If you could create your dream job, what would it look like?"

Once you get yacht-sailing with a bevy of supermodels/sexy firemen out of your system, focus in on the specific aspects of that job that make it so appealing. Do you really enjoy being on the water? Do you like wearing a cap or double-breasted suits? Great! That's your starting point.

Now, take it a step further. Ask around about what sorts of jobs allow an individual to work on or around water, wear suits, and _____ (fill in the blank with your value). Maybe you were meant to work on a cruise ship? How about constructing a few small experiments to check out this hypothesis?

Perhaps you fancy the notion of creating a career where you leave the corporate world behind and work from home. After arranging your life to try this for a week you might find you love the arrangement as much as you thought you would. Fabulous! Or, to the contrary, maybe you realize the reality is far different than the expectation. Take this learning opportunity to reflect on the lessons you've learned. Why did this experiment flop? Too little structure? Too many kids knocking on your office door? Too much temptation from the fridge? Use this information to create a new GPS point and experiment in the adjacent space. This might include backtracking a bit to something with greater structure, but also more comfortable than a traditional office space. Check out the fit on a co-working space and catalog that experience before creating your next experiment.

Relationship facet

If your challenge lies in personal relationships, you'll go about constructing your Single-Facet Departure path the same way. Either you're looking for a new relationship or you'd like to work on an existing one.

If you are currently in a strained relationship you wish to preserve, it could benefit both partners to simultaneously engage in the process of identifying sustaining and draining activities and their associated values. Then together, you can openly discuss the areas of overlap and divergence. Weathered relationships often morph the way long-term careers do. Just because the relationship isn't currently a good fit, doesn't mean it can't undergo honest examination and invigorating modification.

Identifying activities that overlap both partner's values, and which both partners find sustaining, is crucial to creating a mutually satisfying and harmonious relationship. If your significant other hasn't already read this book, get them a copy. When you both reach this point, you'll each have explored your personal sustaining/draining/desire relationship activities and values. Then, you can compare notes.

A word of caution here...

If your relationship is rocky, I highly recommend starting with ONLY the sustaining and desire activities. Leave any discussion of draining activities for later. You should be well on your way to experiencing a happiness up-tick, by sharing mutually agreed upon sustaining and desire activities aligned with common values, before even considering the draining activities.

Each partner can create their own list of relationship-centric values and activities. After the lists are compared in a nonjudgmental fashion, you can both apply your creativity training to brainstorm additional activities aligned with your shared values. Keep this in mind, though: Plan a shared sustaining activity, engage, then reflect! Share another activity, then reflect – together! Are you both still on the same page?

Doesn't this sound romantic?

Values	Activities (Sustaining and Desire)

Social life facet

Perhaps, you've just left college and have an amazing career ahead of you, but you're not sure how to make new friends, and you're really feeling lonely.

Starting from scratch will involve a commitment to Actively learn a new landscape. Fortunately, the internet has made it possible to find numerous different groups of people.

In addition to making new friends, Meetups can be an excellent place to decide whether you might like a new environment or set of tasks or people, with little to no commitment. Attending Meetups allows you to connect with people who already engage in your proposed activities, and with whom you likely share interests.

Use Meetups, or some other group that brings strangers together, as a jumping off point to ask questions and learn more about people and the places they've been. Remember, not all experiments will go as planned. Not every meeting with other people will be comfortable. And when situations don't work out in your favor — reflect! What were your expectations? Did Invulnerability rise from the grave?

Try to bear in mind that even disappointing experiments are rich in lessons.

~~~~~~~~~~~~~~~~~~~~~

CAUTION. Often when you have a clear sense of what you do NOT want (which is often what you currently have or just left behind), it is all too easy to dismiss anything that even slightly resembles it. Try to remain alert to nuances. A tropical rainforest and a temperate deciduous forest are both forests, but each can provide unique experiences. The wildlife is different. The temperature is different. The threat from snakes and bugs are different. You get my drift.

Don't set your GPS coordinates too far from your launching point, at first. Veering from the temperate forest, with nothing but a desert in mind, will likely not only overwhelm you with too many details to process at once, but will block your ability to retain aspects of your current situation that you might actually find sustaining.

Remember the baby and the bath water.

Small experiment... reflect... small experiment... reflect. Ultimately, your repeatedly recalibrated steps might lead you far away from the forest to a distant beach. But, if you take it one step at a time, and reflect on fit, you're way more likely to end up on a beach that will sustain you, rather than one that fits only until the novelty wears off. However, you know your risk tolerance better than I, and I've already owned up to my over-planning nature.

Bottom line... just make sure your steps aren't so broad that it makes reflection and recalibration overwhelming.

~~~~~~~~~~~~~~~~~~~~~

Concrete steps:

1. Identify the draining values and activities for your unfulfilling facet of life.

2. Compare and contrast the values and activities from step 1 with those associated with the fulfilling aspects of your life. Consider how values aligned with the fulfilling facets can inform the creation of sustaining activities associated with the unfulfilling part.

3. Create flexible GPS points based on activities identified in step 2.

4. Continue to craft your path through small experiments designed to assess hypotheses about what you will find sustaining.

CHAPTER 14

The Conscious
Exploration approach

THE KEY TO CREATING a meaningful and fulfilling life path when you're prone to shifting focus away from the process to the destination, is to populate your path with a plethora of sustaining activities that are strongly aligned with your values. By peppering the trail with distracting, value-consistent, sustaining shiny things, you ensure that you do not develop a straight-and-narrow, tunnel-vision path.

If you are a typical Type A person, always driven by competition or an achievement orientation (or both!), you are likely to miss out on the smell of the roses. With your eye on the finish line, you'll miss the simple pleasures of sunsets, the taste of watermelon on a summer day, the crackling of a campfire, your kids' childhoods... Yet some people are just constitutionally driven, it seems. They may not even have demon voices driving them on, they simply are made this way.

Because of the propensity for single-minded focus on outcomes, and the anxiety that often accompanies it, the Zen quote: "You should sit in meditation for 20 minutes a day. Unless you're too busy, then you should sit for an hour," rings true. Is this you? Be honest!

If you are destination-focused and find that the sustaining activities you create for yourself often become draining activities, the Conscious Exploration approach is for you.

You are probably quite Thoughtful and Active in your approach to your lifepath. You may even be very Curious and creative in developing your journey. The problem for Type A driven people is often a deficit of Process appreciation. So, for those of you who are like me, you must strengthen your Process muscles.

How often do you start an endeavor with great verve, commitment, and enthusiasm, only to find a few months later that you are bored or sick of it? Maybe it's not an endeavor, so much as a relationship. Do you enter into romantic relationships with an ideal in mind? Do you work to create this vision only to be let down by partners who ultimately don't meet your expectations or share your end-game vision?

Here's the challenge, as I see it.

Destination people suffer from tunnel vision. Moreover, we often struggle with control. For this reason, we need to ensure we inoculate ourselves against these tendencies. How do we do that? We build a measure of ADD (Attention Deficit Disorder) into our GPS.

Here is the typical destination-driven path to success:

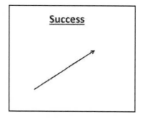

Straight and narrow. No time to mess around. Get it done. Don't stop 'til you drop. Sound familiar? Sound fun? Sound fulfilling? No way! Sound like a path built upon shovel messages? Yup, this IS the recipe for making a sustaining activity into a draining activity.

Here's another well-documented route to success:

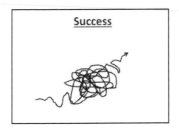

Oh... My... God! That looks so messy and terrible!

But, wait...

It doesn't look boring or draining, does it? In fact, it looks like this route incorporates many different diversions based on Curiosity that would stoke additional insights along the way.

That's pretty awesome.

Before getting started, I'd like you to consider engaging in an exercise I also advocate for the Radical Departure approach. There's a good chance your destination focus is a result, at least in part, of an achievement orientation. Often this is the result of the aforementioned internalized messages that leave you with a need to prove that you are worthy.

Well, if you've experienced this, I have news for you. You matter regardless of what anyone else thinks of you!

Along the way, though, you're going to hear those faint echoes telling you that you're going to miss out on the accolades, and that someone else is going to receive the recognition. The demons will rise from the depths to remind you of how awful that would be.

Now's your chance to construct a rebuttal to that nonsense. Go back and watch Music and Life, if need be. Then write out your response to your most troubling demon. Remember, this can take the form of a "It's not you, it's me" kiss-off speech or a "hands over your ears and eyes shut" mantra. Either way, write out your note to the demon or your new mantra, and refer back to it when you need a reminder that life is about way more than trophies.

_____

_____

_____

_____

_____

_____

_____

_____

_____

_____

_____

The Conscious Exploration approach deliberately incorporates diversions along the path.

For starters, these diversions distract you and give your mind a break from the task at hand. Have you ever noticed how you get your best ideas in the shower, when you're brushing your teeth, or when you're drifting off to sleep? That's because your brain is relaxed and the left side is open to allowing the right side to chime in for a change.

A singular destination focus shuts off the right side of your brain, often cutting Curiosity off at the knees and depriving you of your most interesting insights.

The second reason for the incorporation of distractions and diversions, is to break the monotony. I've heard from folks who work at chocolate shops who say they eventually get sick of chocolate. I know! But, it's true. Same goes for that job or relationship you're currently focused on. So, let's give it some space to breathe.

Your job now is to find additional activities to incorporate into your well-mapped out path.

Risa's path

When I reviewed my draining and sustaining activities and associated values chart, it became apparent that I value helping others learn, operating independently, creativity, engaging in activities that provide me a sense of intellectual challenge, and adventure. I knew that to get me out of my professional slump, my pushpins had to include things that would provide a respite from my daily environment.

In writing this book, I was able to create an endeavor that checked these boxes. The key for me, it turns out, is to ensure I have additional, less-consuming, pushpins along the path to break me away from my tendency to obsessively focus.

In reviewing my charts, I noticed great overlap between my draining activities and my sustaining activities. This tells me that it's easy for me to let satisfying endeavors become all-consuming chores. To guarantee that my path remains fulfilling and satisfying, I have to tack-on diversions and pit stops to ensure I don't burn out the engine by turning enjoyable activities into burdensome responsibilities.

During the process of writing this book, those diversions involved creating a Pinterest board with décor ideas for my son's first apartment, planning a hiking trip to Colorado, and working in my garden. Sure, two out of three of those things involved planning, but they constituted pleasant, minimally invasive distractions that ensured I didn't turn sustaining and fulfilling book-writing into hole-digging, book-writing labor.

In general, if you require a Conscious Explorer approach, you likely tend to resort to autopilot mode after creating a laser-focus on your destination. Like a magnet, you're pulled toward a goal forged of steel. Recognizing this tendency allows you to slow down and think deliberately about the steps involved in reaching your goals. When you do so, you'll be able to build-in respite points.

Then, rather than simply being pulled through the forest to the other side, you can schedule stops that will allow you to take note of scenic vistas, chipmunks, and pretty leaves. Such stops rejuvenate you and prevent the sort of burnout that turns sustaining activities into draining activities.

Charting your path

Let's start by developing your 'distracting activities' list from your List of Things Not to Forget I Enjoy. Classify these by the amount of time they require. You can divide them up any way you'd like, but maybe consider activities under 30 minutes, those from 30 minutes to an hour, and those requiring more than an hour. Be sure to include a variety of activities that require a wide range of time commitments.

<u>Activity</u>   <u>Estimated Time</u>

_____   _____

_____   _____

_____   _____

_____   _____

_____   _____

_____   _____

_____   _____

_____   _____

_____   _____

_____   _____

_____   _____

_____   _____

_____   _____

_____   _____

_____   _____

_____   _____

_____   _____

_____   _____

_____   _____

Next, consider the GPS points you've decided upon for your life path. Contemplate the steps involved in reaching them. Then, start building in some scenic vistas and rest stops that will ensure your path remains an enjoyable journey, rather than an arduous trek to a predetermined destination that loses its luster with each new step.

For the first GPS coordinate, think about the steps required to reach it, and then jot down diversionary activities to engage in at the end of each step. Repeat this process for each unique GPS point you have included along your life journey. Your GPS points might pertain to various facets of your life, but regardless, peripheral activities should be built-in as you progress toward all your goals.

GPS destination point: _____

Steps toward my GPS destination point

1. _____
   _____

   Diversion Activity: _____
   _____

2. _____
   _____

   Diversion Activity: _____
   _____

3. _____
   _____

   Diversion Activity: _____
   _____

4. _____
   _____

   Diversion Activity: _____
   _____

5. _____
   _____

   Diversion Activity: _____
   _____

6. _____

_____

Diversion Activity: _____

_____

During your time engaged in diversionary activities, consider yourself prohibited from thinking about your destination!

I suggest keeping your journal with you during your sustaining diversion activities. If your right brain kicks in with a creative notion or your left brain remembers another competing commitment pertaining to your destination, jot it down and get back to it when you finish your diversionary ice cream cone.

Trying to suppress your thoughts, while enjoying your diversion activity, will not work out well for you. Want proof of this? Okay. Don't think about a white bear. Think about anything else besides polar bears. No Coca-Cola® bears, no baby white bears, no decorative polar bears. Whatcha thinking about now?

Yeah, so keep a journal with you so your mind doesn't continually intrude with "more important stuff."

Concrete steps:

1. Begin by listing out your sustaining and desire activities. Brainstorm until you have at least twenty-five. Estimate how much time each would take.

2. Chart out your path to the next GPS destination you are working toward. List the steps involved in reaching this point.

3. As best you can, chart the steps required to reach each of the broader GPS coordinates on your tentative life path. Once you've identified the steps, build in pit-stops and commit yourself to engaging in these diversionary activities of different time spans all along the way.

4. During your time engaged in diversionary activities, remember to immerse yourself. Enjoy the diversion. Shift your focus back to the diversion, should it drift to your destination.

5. As you continue creating your fulfilling life path, get in the habit of programming in breaks.

6. Remind yourself frequently that all work and no play will make you (and me and Jack) not only dull, but depressed and unfulfilled boys and girls.

CHAPTER 15

Off you go

YOU'VE ACCOMPLISHED a great deal over the past few weeks or months! Now, it's time to start looking into the future and asking some probing questions. Whose story resounded most for you, Cheryl and Elizabeth's, Marin's, Jack's, or mine? Could it be that you and I have in common a tendency to develop a fun-sucking vacuum-sealed path? Will your path help you develop a whole new life for yourself? Will it involve a redirection? Or, will it simply enrich a well-suited current trajectory?

I don't have a fill-in-the-blank exercise for this one. But, by now you know yourself well-enough. You know which facets of your life and your being have been swayed and/or disrupted by societal messages and demon voices echoing in your head. You know how to counter those arguments and stay true to who you genuinely are. You are equipped to create an optimally fulfilling life path. All you need now is the confidence and gumption to do it. It's natural to feel a little anxious at this point. But, please, examine those feelings and thoughts. What might at first strike you as anxiety (simply because you are accustomed to the feeling) might very well actually be excitement. When was the last time you were truly excited about your life? Would you recognize the feeling if you felt it? Well, introspect carefully, 'cause I'm willing to bet that's what you are experiencing right now!

~~~~~~~~~~~~~~~~~~~~~

I'm going to miss you

Wow. You've reached the end of your (hopefully, fulfilling) journey with me. Can you believe it? Your work during our time together has been a trip all its own! I am so thankful you've allowed me to guide you along the way. Of course, you did the heavy lifting and the dirty work. *You* climbed out of the hole, *you* slayed the demons, and *you* charted your new and improved life path. But I had a great time cheering you on and chowing down on the trail mix.

By now your shoes are on and you're ready to chart your path and walk-the-walk. You've got a handful of pushpins and you have four different models of path construction to consider. Now, get down to it and determine the path best suited to you.

To ensure you don't leave anything out, this would be a good time to go back and peruse the notes you've made in the margins of this book or in your journal. You may need a separate page to collect all those thoughts in one visual. I like to use a dry-erase marker and write my thoughts all over my bathroom mirror.

Look at your collection of thoughts. How can you arrange them into various themes? When you do so, what meaning do you make of the themes? What do they say about your growth since page 1? What do you make of the folded pages and highlighted sections? What do they say about who you truly are?

~~~~~~~~~~~~~~~~~~~~~

Take a moment and reflect on your journey and recap your accomplishments. It could be fun to write your answers out in your journal and revisit them in a year. Otherwise, just find a quiet spot and contemplate the following...

1. Which of society's messages did you internalize the deepest? Which ones really get you digging?

2. At what point did you realize you were stuck in a hole?

3. Of all the things you missed out on or risked missing out on by being stuck in your hole, which hit you the hardest?

4. Which of the four demons pestered you the most on your way here?

5. Which *personal* values did you previously attend to the least? Which *demon-driven* value held you back the most?

6. Of all the sustaining activities you've incorporated and combined, which align closest with your values? Where and when will you work them into your ongoing journey?

7. What approach will your path take? Weeded out and reconceptualized new path construction? Destination unknown joyful wandering? Recalibrated and re-energized redirection? Sanity-saving roses-smelling frequent-bathroom-breaks trek toward a penciled-in destination? Or, something uniquely your own?

You've done a great deal of work, haven't you? You deserve a pat on the back, for sure. Just remember how easy it is to fall into old habits. Remain aware of your surroundings. Remember, your path is not set in concrete. You are free to roam, take diversions, and scrap it all for something new and exciting at any point no matter what anyone else thinks about it. Check in with yourself and reassess your behaviors in light of your values. Make certain you are remaining true to your nature.

Can I call you "friend?"

I know I don't know you. But, over the past year or so as I've developed this book, I feel like I *have* come to know you. Maybe I took to heart more than I thought, the advice my friend gave me in the beginning to get to know my audience. I hope you feel as though you've come to know me, as well. Can we keep in touch? Will you share your journey with me and stop by to see me when you can? I'd love to catch up.

Feel free to drop me a line at Risa@GenuineU.com and connect on LinkedIn. I'd love to hear from you. Check out my other work at http://www.GenuineU.org.

Goodbye, friend. Go and live your best damn life.

ACKNOWLEDGMENTS

"With my tribe by my side, I will make this shit happen."

— Risa

Writing a book isn't easy. There were plenty of times when I felt defeated and wondered why I'd created such a stupid and torturous new path. But, the above quote hangs over my computer and while toiling away, I referred to it often. Had it not been for my family and friends, I certainly wouldn't have made it to completion. Far from being a stupid and torturous journey, writing the *Best Damn Life Workbook* has been very fulfilling.

My friend, Jennifer Wilding, offered the feedback I presented in the Preface. She was spot on and I definitely owe her for such a candid and helpful critique. Other friends, Theresa Gray, Darrel Lauderdale, Michael Rutherford, Doc Bates, Bernice DenBiesen Whalley, Joe Young, and Abby Mason provided constructive criticism that encouraged me to move forward. I also owe a debt of gratitude to my high school friend, Chris Roush, who graciously applied his journalism skills to help make this book far more interesting than it was originally.

My SCORE mentor John Molish was very tactful in telling me my early titles didn't cut it. My editor, Maria D'Marco was so kind and sweet that I didn't mind her extensive mark-ups.

Mostly, I need to thank the 50-something agents who told me the book's concept and my writing were great but that they wouldn't represent it. That was just what I needed (once I got past the disappointment) to forge ahead. Many days I was driven by little more than spite. But, hey, it did the trick.

And, I am thankful to you, new friend, for sticking with me, too.

Best of luck to you.

ABOUT THE AUTHOR

RISA STEIN earned her PhD in clinical psychology from the University of Memphis back in the old days when it was still Memphis State. Risa is the author of over 60 professional articles and has been quoted in *Psychology Today, Women's Health,* and *Reader's Digest.* Aside from Tennessee, where she completed her undergraduate and graduate work, Risa has lived in New Jersey, Illinois, Georgia, Texas, and Oregon. These days, you can usually find her at home in Kansas City with her family and their two hypoallergenic dogs.

Risa would love to hear from you at:
Risa@GenuineU.com

You can find out more about Risa and her other mental health endeavor GenuineU at:
http://www.GenuineU.org

Notes

Notes

Made in the USA
Columbia, SC
24 May 2019